GOVERNMENT IS KILLING THE ECONOMY!

The Economic Impact of Regulation
and Government Mismanagement on
the U.S. Economy – Common Sense
Thoughts on Finding A Cure

WALTER RAQUET

The graphics on pages 75 to 80 are used with permission of the author of the Grant Thornton report.

ISBN: 978-0-9961947-6-1

DEDICATION

This book is dedicated to Andrew Walter Raquet, 1969-2014.
I love you, Andrew.

CONTENTS

PREFACE

The purpose of this book is to show how all of us can come together and fix the core problems so that we can enjoy a better future. I aim to educate the reader about the dangers of unnecessary regulation and its costly impact. This is neither a Democratic nor a Republican issue. Both parties are guilty. Discussions about who's more at fault are a waste of time and only help to ensure that nothing ever gets done. Public trust in government is at an all-time low of 24 percent. And it is time to make significant changes. Democratic and Republican business executives must unite and help shape policies to take our country back to its former success. Government policies should inspire individuals to become successful entrepreneurs and grow the economy, and it's tragic to see regulation discouraging entrepreneurship and inhibiting growth.

The reason I choose to write this book is my love for this great country. I am sick and tired hearing negative conversation, receiving emails, and watching the chattering pundits of the media complaining about how badly and inefficiently our government is performing. God blessed me with an ability to solve problems and I want to use that talent to help right the ship.

Business people create 100 percent of the jobs and pay 100 percent of the taxes along with their employees. Government is a result of taxpayers contributing their hard-earned dollars to pay for the cost of running the United States of America. Our leaders should spend those dollars carefully to provide the services that are necessary to run our country successfully. These public servants are put in a position of trust to manage the finances of government carefully and efficiently. They do not spend our money carefully nor wisely. I believe that as a group they are doing a very poor job, and that we need to work together to make our government great.

Walter Raquet

"Am I the only guy in this country who's fed up with what's happening? Where the hell is our outrage? We should be screaming bloody murder. We've got a gang of clueless bozos steering our ship of state right over a cliff,..."[1] – Lee Iacocca, Where Have All The Leaders Gone? (Scribner, 2007)

Chapter 1
WHERE WE ARE, HOW WE GOT HERE, AND WHAT TO DO ABOUT IT

Slow growth is the overriding economic issue of our time. "The middle class has not had a raise in 15 years. From 1950 to 2000, the U.S. economy grew at an average rate of 3.5 percent per year. Since 2000, it has grown at half that rate, 1.7 percent,"[2] according to economist John H. Cochrane. Here's how important that is for the middle class: Larry Kudlow, the economist and CNBC host adds: "From 1952 to 2000, real income per person in the U.S. rose from $16,000 to $50,000. But as Cochrane notes, if the American economy grew by only 2 percent per year over that period, rather than 3.5 percent, real incomes for the average person

---

[1] Iacocca, Lee. "Where have all the Leaders Gone?" 2007. http://www.snopes.com/politics/soapbox/iacocca.asp

[2] Cochrane, John H. "Economic Growth." *The Grumpy Economist,* 27 Oct 2015. http://faculty.chicagobooth.edu/john.cochrane/research/papers/cochrane_growth.html

would have risen to only $23,000, not $50,000. That's *huge*. So with less than 2 percent growth in the last 15 years, real-income progress has been stopped."[3]

The reader should be pleased to know that our federal government employees did not have to suffer. On average they received 2 percent more each year than the working middle class. Our politicians took care of their own. Who will ever take care of us?

The middle class has not had a raise in 15 years. As I will show in this book, based on my personal experience and research, government regulations, the inefficient presidential (Bush and Obama) administrations, and out-of-control spending are to blame. Could you imagine if a company gave its employees a rulebook that was 20,000 pages long, as the U.S. did with Obamacare?[4] What about 74,000? (For the IRS). If a business did this it would fail almost immediately. Yet, that's exactly what happened with Obamacare and the tax code, the poster children of over-regulation. How could one person possibly understand or even read the equivalent of 148 500-page books? Regulations this complex make compliance a nightmare. Annually, regulation costs the United States itself $2.028 trillion.[5] The destruction caused by regulation to the American economy is likely higher. An April 2016 working paper from the Mercatus Center at George Mason University shows that regulation has cost the U.S. economy 0.8 percent of lost growth per year since 1980, and that our economy

---

[3] Kudlow, Lawrence
[4] 20,000 Pages of Obamacare Regulations
[5] Cost of Federal Regulations – National Association of Manufacturers

would have been 25 percent larger in 2012 – that's $4 trillion or $13,000 per capita bigger – minus this excess regulation.[6]

To better put this in perspective, the Federal government collects $3.5 trillion in taxes each year, and forces businesses to spend more than $2 trillion on mostly useless regulation enacted by some of the most incompetent politicians and bureaucrats in the world. I believe if we had efficient regulation, the $2 trillion annual cost of existing regulations could be reduced by 75 percent, and that $1.5 trillion saved would flow back into the economy. In addition to increased earnings for workers, we would eliminate most of the harmful effects that bad regulation has on the economy, which could easily be another $2 trillion a year – $4 trillion according to Mercator. Think of the positive impact that stimulus of $3.5 trillion – or $5.5 trillion – a year could have on the economy and the lives of working Americans.

The government isn't all that good at collecting those $3.5 trillion in taxes. Demos.org estimated in March 2011 that tax evasion cost the government about $300 billion a year between 2001 and 2010 – about $3.09 trillion in total, or almost as much as the IRS takes in one year! Essentially, our inefficient federal tax collector lets a full year's revenue get lost every decade.

This book explores in-depth ideas for a better America. The U.S. government has an obligation to act in the best interests of the people it represents. My solution, which I will outline in detail, is to run the Federal government like a business, with a board of directors comprised of half Democratic and Republican business executives and industry experts for every government agency. After

---

[6] Bentley Coffey, Patrick A. McLaughlin and Pietro Peretto, "The Cumulative Cost of Regulations" – http://mercatus.org/sites/default/files/Coffey-Cumulative-Cost-Regs-v3.pdf

presenting more detail on the problem, I will discuss this plan in depth in Chapter 4.

The concept is simple, Each board would hire consultants with relevant expertise to assist them in their work. They would apply the best and most efficient business practices to a failing and wasteful system. They would be able to hire and fire and trim obsolete rules and functions. A lack of accountability in government is perpetuating inefficiency, harmful and needless regulations and strangling our businesses, with no real progress or repercussion.

Let's be clear. I'm no doomsayer. The U.S. is the greatest country, the world's largest economy. However, our true potential as a country is stunted by costly regulations, compromised politicians and blatant government waste. Given all the progress in productivity we've made with new technology and global communications, American business should be soaring. It's not. Our government is holding us back. In this book I am going to detail the destructive nature of an unchecked government and how we can fix it.

The areas negatively affected by government are endless, including business creation, education, employment, capital markets, energy, and immigration. Everything is connected, but the engine only runs when you allow people to innovate, create, and benefit from their efforts without government interference and hindrance. The U.S. Federal government is the biggest single employer in the country, creating and providing goods and services just like a large company. Yet it's run like anything but. When government makes mistakes, the overwhelming tendency is to simply raise taxes or enforce restrictive business regulations to mask their misconduct, fostering more unemployment and hurting the middle class.

A strong, vibrant economy enables the taxpayer to provide the government with funding to ensure our safety, the promise of acting in the best interest of the people, and yes, to protect the environment. President Barack Obama has cited climate change as the number one issue of today, but I challenge his opinion. In my view, over-regulation is the number one threat to the health of the United States because it prevents businesses from adding employees and is denying our youth the opportunities we seniors have enjoyed.

If you don't believe me, how about the opinion of 1,400 CEOs? According to Dennis Nally, chairman of PricewaterhouseCoopers: "Without question chief executive confidence levels are down in a very significant way year to year." The tax-consulting group just did a study, released on the eve of the World Economic Forum in Davos, Switzerland in January 2016. Their annual survey of CEOs in 83 countries showed the key threat CEOs believe they must contend with is over-regulation. Fully 79 percent of the business leaders said they were being stifled by government regulation. This was the number one concern. [7]

Shortly down the list of other concerns, but still in the 70th percentile among the CEOs, were:

- Availability of key skilled labor, which represents a failure of our education system to prepare students with the skills they need to succeed.

---

[7] USA Today Article Money 1/19/16
http://www.usatoday.com/story/money/2016/01/19/pwc-ceo-survey-davos-world-economic-forum/78991930/

- The government response to fiscal deficit and debt burden, because unchecked spending results in mortgaging our future.

- The increasing tax burden makes some countries, such as the U.S., which has the highest rates, uncompetitive with many others and encourages companies to leave the U.S. and go to countries with lower rates.

As I will show, getting rid of harmful regulation and running government agencies like businesses would go a long way toward solving these problems, too. Businesses create 100 percent of our jobs, but our government will not listen to the needs of business leaders. The real victims are the hard-working middle class. It is a travesty that we are denying Millennials the opportunities we enjoyed. The politicians are the only ones to blame. They destroy the economy and inhibit job creation, killing our chances for a better future.

There's a political price as well. *The Wall Street Journal*, in a March 28, 2016 editorial entitled "Why Americans Hate Government," cited the case of Decker College, a for-profit college that was essentially hounded out of business a decade ago, only to be vindicated recently. The Education Department found that a government regulatory council had falsely said the college wasn't accredited when it actually was.

Over-regulation is a classic case of government incompetence. All government regulations must be measured carefully and their impact on the economy must be disclosed. We cannot trust this task to the government. It must be measured independently by a group of industry experts, both Democratic and Republican. How could this work? The new Board of Directors would review all proposed and current regulation and decide whether it makes sense. They would then modify it or eliminate it. These changes would be made in conjunction with Congress.

Democratic and Republican business executives, as well as independent experts, must unite and help shape policies to take our country back. Individuals should be inspired to become successful entrepreneurs because government policies encourage them to do so. Current regulation discourages entrepreneurism, which is tragic. I want to educate the reader about government and the dangers of costly unnecessary regulation and its impact.

I speak about this from experience: As an entrepreneur I created Knight/Trimark Group two decades ago, and it was one of the fastest growing companies in history. I would not be able to create that company today. Excessive regulation ended that opportunity forever. Because of this, we must get rid of job killing regulation. I believe we must improve the way our government works before it is too late.

I feel I am qualified to give such advice, having accomplished the following in my life:

- I became an entrepreneur in 1995 and founded Knight Trimark Group Inc., a company with $17 million and 70 employees. With a lot of hard work and a favorable business environment, Knight became one of the fastest-growing companies in history. In its fifth year, the company had earnings before taxes (EBITDA) of $301 million, employed 1400 people, and was valued at $8 billion at its high.

- In 1997, I predicted the terrible harm that an asinine regulation by former SEC Chairman Arthur Levitt would bring to U.S. capital markets, but unfortunately my 11 letters about how harmful this was were ignored. Eighteen million jobs were lost over a 15-year period directly because of his Order Handling and Best Execution rules.[8] Consultants Grant Thornton issued a report in 2012 that confirmed this.

- In 1980, I uncovered a $1 billion tax fraud, then the largest fraud in the history of the United States, and I assisted the U.S. Treasury and the IRS in shutting it down.

- In 1984, along with two associates I created the first sophisticated equity trading system, called COLT, that was used by the majority of the world's trading firms.

- At the age of 71, I am working closely with the CEO of a clean air company, AtmosAir.com, that we plan to grow to a multi-billion dollar enterprise in the next few years.

We'll start with a look at the three biggest problems I see. The first is uncontrolled and unexamined government waste, the second is public and private fraud, and the third and most important is over-regulation as embodied by the 74,000 pages of regulations and commentary on them comprising the U.S. Tax Code and the 20,000 pages of Obamacare. Another area where regulations stifle growth is our tangle of immigration laws. This is a hot-button issue on both left and right, but I'll argue that regardless of whether we build walls or grant citizenship to millions of people, we need to target the most-productive group of immigrants. New immigrants should be chosen based on their ability to contribute to society in a positive, lasting way.

---

[8]Weild, David, Edward Kim, and Lisa Newport. "The Trouble With Small Tick Sizes." Grant Thornton, LLP. September 2012. http://www.grantthornton.com/staticfiles/GTCom/Public%20companies%20an d%20capital%20markets/Trouble_Small_Ticks.pdf

Then I'll offer specific solutions to these problems, focused on creating bi-partisan boards of directors for all government departments and agencies, and establishing an effective program to encourage and reward whistleblowers that would stamp out waste and fraud. Including business executives and industry experts in the conversation will increase efficiency and remove waste. All politicians talk about cutting waste, fraud, and abuse in government programs during their campaigns for office, but nothing happens once they get elected. I'll show exactly how a board of directors will take care of this problem in short order. Business executives hate waste and will not tolerate its continuation.

Some of the least-discussed regulations are those that perpetuate the system. Government officials and employees enjoy special privileges that they've granted themselves. Public employee unions use taxpayer dollars to lobby government officials, and contribute to the campaigns of politicians who will extract even more money from overburdened taxpayers. Getting rid of the rules that allow this is essential.

Who is lobbying for the taxpayer? The answer we have is no one. The only power we have is our right to vote for candidates who will grow the economy and not the government.

Whistleblowers are one of businesses' least-appreciated – and often reviled, fired or jailed – resources for exposing fraud. After all, these are the people working with the wrongdoers who really know what's going on. They need to be incentivized and rewarded for reporting wrongdoing. This will prove to be a huge deterrent, at a minimal cost. I'll show exactly how this can be done. We'll examine the largest financial frauds in recent years, some of which were exposed by whistleblowers, and see, counter-intuitively, how they could have been prevented by LESS regulation. Prior to 2011 there were no rules and potential whistleblowers would need costly legal advice and were not protected from prosecution. I'll show how an industry-designed whistleblower program can stop hundreds of these frauds, many going on right now, without imposing yet more costly regulations. I'll tell the story for the first time of how I helped expose one of the biggest financial frauds in history.

I have been a proponent of a whistleblower program since 1982. On May 25, 2011, the SEC finally enacted such a program. It's still inadequate but better than nothing. I'll say more about it later. So much waste could be eliminated with a business-like program that rooted out fraud. Regulations could be eliminated. Sarbanes-Oxley could go for sure. It took our government 30 years to get this whistleblower program done. We need now to get rid of all the unnecessary impediments to making it a success. No doubt my proposed boards of directors would see the value in whistleblower programs throughout the government. They need to become the norm for private companies as well.

Both of these initiatives – the boards and the whistleblower programs -- would cut red tape, cut government spending, free up businesses to operate more efficiently and create more jobs. You would be shocked at what adding a board of directors for each government agency, and letting the government employees who see waste and fraud be incentivized to report it without fear, would accomplish.

Then we'll do a deeper dive into two cases with which I'm very familiar:

- From 1998 until 2002, over-regulation of the NASDAQ Stock Market destroyed the then-burgeoning market for initial public offerings, or IPOs, which had been the lifeblood of the job-creating technology sector. This cost

18 million jobs and is still hurting job creation every year. I will argue this is because of over-regulation, and as we've seen getting rid of a lot of these rules will unleash the world's greatest job-creation engine again.

- Then I'll tell you the story of Knight, a company I helped found that revolutionized Wall Street despite the tangle of regulation, and hope that many of these rules that stand in our way today will be eliminated to make it possible for you to do what I did at Knight, and let thousands of innovative companies flourish.

Following on the Knight story, we'll look at how regulations are particularly damaging to the 40-and-under group who have a net worth equal to half of what their parents had when they were at the same age. There are over 781,000 articles about Millennials falling behind their parents in wealth accumulation. I'll offer real solutions and hope for them. After that, I'll offer a few stories of entrepreneurship that I've been involved with as guideposts for the future.

Closing out this section, I'll offer some tips on encouraging entrepreneurship in a new era of fewer regulations. Throughout my career I have learned a lot about what makes a person successful. I want to pass my thoughts about success to the readers at the end of this book. One thought for now is that I always approached my job with the attitude that, "If I were the company president how would I make the company more efficient?" The president needs to know how everything works, so I always tried to understand all the various components of the business. If you do not know something, do not be afraid to say you do not know it. Credibility and integrity are critical to success. The phonies get weeded out very fast, although sometimes not fast enough.

We'll end with a look back and ahead to making this country even greater than it is by changing the rules.

So join me as we look in detail at how to fix what's wrong in the greatest country on Earth so we can continue creating a future of optimism. Let's get started.

"It will be of little avail to the people that the laws are made by men of their own choice if the laws be so voluminous that they cannot be read, or so incoherent that they cannot be read, or so incoherent that they cannot be understood." – James Madison.

Chapter 2
THE PROBLEM, PART 1: OVER-REGULATION

The popular website Business Insider listed 12 Ridiculous Government Regulations That Are Almost Too Bizarre to Believe in November 2010. These include the state of Texas requiring every computer repair technician to obtain a private investigator's license; a Federal law that says Amish farmers can't sell raw milk on their farms; and a report that a U.S. District Court fined a Massachusetts fisherman $500 for releasing a whale trapped in his nets instead of calling and waiting for state officials to come cut the creature free. Additionally, the Food and Drug Administration created rules mandating the food service industry spend an additional 14 million man-hours a year on adding calorie counts to all their vending machines. The rules embedded in Obamacare, which we'll discuss further later on, require small businesses to file millions more 1099 tax forms a year, an average of 200 more per business.

These and many, many other regulations constantly waste the time of businesses, small and large alike, who need to hire staff or hire outside consultants to comply with them all, generating literally tons of paper or billions of bytes of information that nobody's ever going to need or use.

Why is this so? Ask any businessperson and they'll tell you it's pointless, that it largely doesn't do much to protect the consumer or their employees because it's in their economic interest not to do anything that would harm either. Are some of the rules needed? Of course, but often there is no appeal or repeal process, so outdated regulations live forever. Ask any government employee why the rules are the way they are and you'll get in reply nothing more than a shrug or "that's above my pay grade."

By far the most plentiful and harmful regulations in all of government reside in the Treasury Department, specifically in the Internal Revenue Service. It won't do much good to prune the 74,000 pages of largely incomprehensible regulations that have spawned a sprawling network of lawyers and accountants and consultants and special interests that keep getting Congress and the IRS to churn them out. They need to be cleared out wholesale.

This is a political issue, one that's being discussed by people of all political persuasions. In my opinion, what needs to happen – and can happen – is to adopt a far simpler tax code, trash nearly all those regulations, and cut the IRS down to size or eliminate it altogether. Doing this could actually increase total tax revenue while giving most people and companies a tax cut, and create millions of jobs. All of the Republican presidential candidates have proposed exactly that. There is significant support in Congress for some sort of simplified system.

Let's give our country's tax issue some historical context.

According to a piece by Matthew K. Burke entitled "It's Time to Abolish the IRS and Adopt the Fair Tax," on the website The

Politistick in April 2015, the Federal income tax was established in 1913. At that time, the tax return was one page, and the entire tax code was 14 pages. Federal income tax was set at a minimum tax of 1 percent and maximum tax of 7 percent on the extremely wealthy. A provision was originally considered to prevent government from being able to raise the income tax rate above 10 percent, but the provision was tossed out as it was considered too "outlandish."

"Now the top rate has reached 39.6 percent, which is almost four times the rate considered an outrageous impossibility by those who created the original provision," Burke writes. "Today, with more than 74,000 pages of largely incomprehensible income tax regulations – burdensome, unproductive compliance costs of more than $300 billion annually."

Writing in *The Wall Street Journal* of Dec. 29, 2014, John Steele Gordon, author of *"An Empire of Wealth: The Epic History of American Economic Power,"* (HarperCollins, 2004), listed 10 reasons to abolish the corporate income tax. Among them:

- *As the tax is abolished,* "with it disappears an army of lobbyists in Washington working to get favorable tax treatment for corporations.

- "With no corporate income tax, management would concentrate on what is now pretax profits, an artifact of actual wealth creation.

- "(W)ith suddenly increased profits, corporations would increase both dividends and investment in plant and equipment, with very positive effects for the economy as a whole and increased revenue to the government through the personal income tax.

- "(M)uch of the $2 trillion of foreign earnings, now kept abroad to avoid being taxed when repatriated, would flow into this country. That would greatly increase the country's liquid capital. That, in turn, would cause interest rates to decline and investment in plant and equipment and new technology to go up, boosting the economy as a whole, and thus federal revenues."

Forbes added another reason to Gordon's list: Companies themselves actually pay no tax. Anything they pay is passed on to customers in higher prices or to shareholders in lower dividends.

Not to get too far ahead of ourselves, but I mentioned boards of directors as a central part of my solution to the problems of over-regulation and government waste, and I'll discuss this in detail in Chapter 4. But for now, imagine the Treasury Board led by Bill Gates and Chuck Lee (former CEO of GTE and Verizon) going over the latest recommendations from the regulation task force that has identified roughly 50,000 regulations that can now be erased because of the new President's tax plans. Mary Barra from General Motors and Tim Cook of Apple go over plans to all but eliminate business taxes and allow companies to repatriate their overseas earnings. Representatives from H&R Block and TurboTax unveil the new, shorter form 1040.

Although the above is unthinkable in our present system, it isn't a pipe dream. We must simplify the tax code. Business taxes account for less than 10 percent of revenues, yet these businesses create nearly 100 percent of our country's jobs. Why not have ZERO business tax? We are in a highly competitive world economy; therefore, we must create the best possible environment for business to thrive. Politicians refuse to use logic. Lots of companies are shifting operations overseas to countries where there are more favorable tax rates. We are in a competition with the world. Politicians cannot make decisions in a vacuum; that's why we need business people to help them.

U.S. corporate income tax contributes only 1.8 percent of GDP (equivalent to $288 billion in 2013), according to a research paper by Hans Fehr, Sabine Jokish, Ashwin Kambhampati and Laurence J. Kotlikoff. This pales in comparison to the cost of collecting this tax, which by some estimates is as much as $300 billion a year. Worse yet, America features a relatively high marginal business tax rate of 35 percent, according to the Tax Foundation, which encourages both U.S. and foreign corporations to keep operations and an estimated total of more than $2.1 trillion in profits offshore. Apple alone had more than $181 billion parked offshore in 2014 according to a study by Citizens for Tax Justice and the Public Interest Research Group Education Fund.

Worse yet, governments abroad are making changes to protect their people in terms of corporate tax collection. Here at home, we continue to allow a marginal tax rate that is among the highest of the developed countries, and just sit by and watch while others lower their rates. A high rate encourages American companies like Apple to operate overseas and prevents American companies from returning overseas profits and reinvesting them domestically. That $2.1 trillion of profits held by the largest 500 U.S. companies overseas is depriving the Treasury of an estimated $620 billion in revenue. Think of the stimulus repatriating that money and collecting those taxes would unleash, among other things reducing the budget deficit.

Why does the public not care? There is an important misconception that needs to be corrected. The general public believes that corporate income tax is paid by rich owners of large companies and that it does not affect workers. In reality, it is the U.S. worker who bears this tax burden because high corporate income tax leads companies to move abroad and employ people outside of the U.S. That leaves Americans who are looking for work at a huge disadvantage. Corporate tax drives investment out of our country, which is detrimental, with a surprisingly small benefit in terms of government revenue, which could easily be found elsewhere.

Meanwhile, awash in all those regulations, the IRS fails to collect around $300 billion in money lost to tax fraud a year. For many of the past ten years this amount has actually exceeded the total collected from corporations, according to the Tax Foundation.

It is unimaginable that a business, with a competent board of directors, would fail to collect $300 billion in accounts receivable each year. This is sheer incompetence on the part of the IRS. And it's not just lost revenue. The IRS pays out about $5.8 billion in fraudulent refunds each year, according to Robert W. Wood writing in Forbes in February 2015. This is a classic failure of the accounts payable overseers. How could this happen? They do not check the taxpayer's address or verify that the taxpayer earned the money or paid the taxes. For example, a college student in Stamford, Conn. makes $5,000 at a summer job. An identity thief steals his information and creates a W-2 for $100,000.00 with lots of tax withheld and files for a refund of $5,000. The IRS pays it without checking to see if the W-2 is legitimate and that the person's address is the same. Is the IRS operating in the Stone Age?

In effect, yes. The IRS does not use the technology that is readily available today by businesses. Online brokers can process complex trades in seconds. To help collect those $300 billion in unpaid taxes, they could easily assemble a database of all taxpayers and the property they own, their brokerage and bank accounts, credit card spending and automobiles they own. They could estimate how much a person would have to make in order to have all of these assets and compare that number to the income declared. They could catch a large number of tax cheats. Is this too intrusive? Maybe not. Your bank and credit card companies already know all this stuff, and privacy protections could be put in place.

Has the IRS been starved of enough enforcement agents because of Congressional budget cuts? Is that why they leave so much uncollected? Perhaps, but again, not getting too far ahead of ourselves, this is exactly what business analysts hired on short-term contracts by my proposed board of directors would figure out, and recommend hiring the most cost-effective number. And they'd have the right technology to do their jobs.

How did the IRS regulation get to a staggering 74,000 pages? It's simple. Lobbyists are paid handsomely to convince government officials to do special favors for their companies or unions. The paperwork grows and grows, and not to the benefit of the average worker. We are living in a corrupt world.

Let's take a look at just one such case of relatively new regulations. A report from consultants Dixon Hughes Goodman in December 2013 detailed more than 100 pages of fresh regulations governing "the treatment of materials and supplies, capitalization of amounts paid to acquire or produce tangible property and the capitalization and deduction of expenditures relating to repair or improvement of tangible property." In other words, building materials. The Dixon Hughes report itself has five pages of recommendations for small business owners, which attempt to explain the new complexities the IRS is adding. No reasons are given as to how this will help businesses, probably because they won't, and no cost-benefit analysis is offered. Could a small-business owner figure out this stuff herself without hiring a consultant? No way.

And then there's the Patient Protection and Affordable Care Act of 2010, also known as Obamacare, which in 20,000 pages of rules and regulations transformed a sixth of our economy. This has become a highly politicized issue, with Democrats passing it into law when they held a super-majority in the Senate and a majority in the House of Representatives, and Republicans voting to repeal it more than 50 times since they regained House control.

Leaving the politics aside, let's just look at a few of these new regulations. Townhall.com reported in November 2015 that because all restaurant chains with more than 20 locations nationwide have to post calorie information for each menu item, craft breweries, which typically don't calculate calorie accounts for the varieties of beer they brew, would now need to furnish such information or the restaurants wouldn't be able to sell their beer to those chains. The website cites a Cato Institute study that shows that complying with this regulation can cost a small brewer up to $77,000, which many can't afford. Never mind that other studies show calorie counts matter little to beer drinkers! This regulation does not help anyone, but could put a small but popular segment of brewers out of business. A board of directors would understand this and put a stop to this useless regulation.

Obamacare is a complicated tangle of rules and regulations, many of which have already been changed by Congress and executive order because they just didn't work. Some rules for requiring businesses to cover their employees or pay a fine have been changed, some several times, as has the infamous individual mandate requiring everyone to have insurance or pay a tax penalty. It's a layer of complexity added to an already overly complex system, that nobody, even the rapidly expanding ranks of lawyers and accountants springing up around the law, understands.

We must simplify things. One way would be to replace our present system of many tax rates and many deductions with a graduated flat tax of 10 percent on the first $60,000 of income and

20 percent to 25 percent after that. No deductions! This would automatically be more efficient and benefit everyone. And we could vastly reduce or eliminate the IRS. While this is my favored approach, there are many variations, including several offered by Republican presidential candidates in 2016. A quick Google search offers 229,000 articles on the graduated flat tax. We need to take the best ideas and implement them.

We also have to simplify the business tax code. Business taxes account for less than 10 percent of revenues, yet companies create nearly 100 percent of the jobs. Why not eliminate the business tax? We are in a highly competitive world economy. We must create the best possible environment for businesses to thrive. With a graduated flat tax on people, according to nearly all models, government revenue would increase enough to make this revenue from businesses irrelevant. But it's plenty relevant to business of all sizes that could use the savings to hire more people, give them all a raise, or otherwise expand their operations, creating millions of jobs.

Politicians refuse to see what's actually happening because they refuse to change the system. (Perhaps they're too busy doing nothing. A recent *60 Minutes* report revealed that of the 120 days a year our nations congressmen and -women are supposed to be on the job in Washington, they spend half their time calling donors looking for money.) Every day the newspapers and Internet offer stories of companies shifting operations overseas to countries where there are more favorable tax rates. Some are letting themselves be "acquired" by foreign companies, even though the U.S. company will remain dominant in the merger. This is a phenomenon known as "tax inversion" which does nothing more than cut tax revenue properly owed to the U.S. by some of the biggest and most profitable companies in our country. This needs to be stopped.

Politicians must wake up to reality. We are in competition with the world. Politicians cannot make decisions in a vacuum, that's why we need business people to help them, as we'll see in Chapter 4.

Take the crucial issue of immigration. Setting aside for a moment the problem of some 12 million people already in this country without documents, our system of regulations that's grown up around immigration is a mess and a disgrace. According to an April, 2015 report by the Center for Immigration Studies, more than 4.4 *million* people are on legal waiting lists to get into the U. S. The waiting times for normal processing can run from two years to 33 years for some categories. More than half are people who have been sponsored by family members who are already U.S. citizens, For this favored group, the waiting time is a stunning 13 years. For Mexicans, it is 18 years. Aside from the issue of whether this encourages illegal immigration, waiting times like this aren't just matters of law. They are evidence of sloppiness, inefficiency, and lack of modern technology.

Countries thrive based on the intellectual talent that they have. We educate thousands of the best and brightest and then force them to leave after graduation. If we were running the country like a business we would keep the best talent, and we could certainly get the waiting times way down for these immigrants with proper computers and databases and more and better-trained immigration workers.

About ten years ago I heard a politician say something brilliant. He said that the U.S. should allow 1 million immigrants in annually, but "only the best and brightest." He went on to say that they would be employed or create businesses and it would be unlikely that would commit crimes or be on welfare. That individual was Rahm Emanuel, a Democrat and now the mayor of

Chicago. I agree with him. We should not have people immigrating to America only to go on public assistance.

Our immigration mess is really a story of regulation gone awry. We have a whole body of unnecessary regulations that do exactly the opposite of what we want, in part by encouraging people we don't want to come in illegally and discouraging people we do want from coming in legally. It's not that surprising when you realize that immigration is governed by separate sets of thousands of regulations each by the Department of Homeland Security, the State Department, the Department of Justice, the Department of Labor, and the Department of Health and Human Services. No wonder there is a thriving and woefully overmatched network of immigration lawyers, expediters and enforcers. And no wonder it can take up to 33 years!

As we'll see in Chapter 4, a board of directors for Homeland Security charged with, among other things, reorganizing the Immigration and Naturalization Service along basic business lines would slash regulations and waiting times. The whistleblower reward program I detail in Chapter 5 would also help, policing employer abuses and cutting down on illegal immigration once the legal impediments have been cleaned up.

But even more could be done immediately. There exist special visas called H-1B, EB-1, EB-2, and EB-5 that let in extraordinarily talented individuals, Ph.D.s in some fields, and business people who have $500,000 to invest in a business in the U.S. But there aren't enough of any of these categories (and half a million dollars is way too high) and Silicon Valley high-tech companies regularly complain that the rules prevent them from hiring all the engineers they need to expand and create even more jobs. Indian and Chinese graduates are the biggest recipients of coveted H-1B visas, which are limited to 85,000 a year. In 2015 this cap was reached in five days after applications were opened.

This is a no-brainer. Let the best people in!

In the past, immigrants or children of immigrants have greatly enriched our lives. From the Pilgrims to Albert Einstein to Steve Jobs, we are truly a nation of immigrants. Let's embrace our heritage and benefit from the fact that we are the greatest and most attractive country on Earth to further enhance our future. All it takes is sweeping the bureaucrats and their regulations out of the way.

But aren't we already too crowded and wouldn't more immigrants just take more jobs away from already hard-pressed American workers?

Not so, said the Cato Institute in a study of various reports in 2104. Employment and wages for U.S.-born workers varied little as legal immigration has increased. Between 2010 and 2014 immigrants accounted for about 2 million new jobs, but native-born American employment grew by 4.7 million jobs in that same period.

We actually need more people to ensure that we can grow faster than the 2 percent year we seem to be stuck at since the 2007-2008 recession. The U.S. population grew by less than 1 percent in 2015 for the third straight year, and the fertility rate (the number of babies per couples of child-bearing age) grew by under 2 percent for the first time since 1990. Because the rate is below the replacement rate of two per couple, our small population growth is being entirely fed by immigrants. We can afford and indeed need more immigrants paying taxes and helping our economy grow.

A 2015 report by the Hoover Institution cited studies showing that immigration between 1990 and 2007 actually raised everyone's real incomes by 6.6 percent to 9.9 percent. The Federal Reserve

Bank of San Francisco found in 2010 that immigrants "expand the country's productive capacity by stimulating investment and promoting specialization." Let's get rid of silly rules, increase tax revenue, lift the burden of red tape from business, let the best people in, and watch our economy take off to the benefit of us all.

"It is a popular delusion that the government wastes vast amounts of money through inefficiency and sloth. Enormous effort and elaborate planning are required to waste this much money."
P. J. O'Rourke, Parliament of Whores

Chapter 3

THE PROBLEM, PART 2: WASTE AND INEFFICIENCY, AND SELF-PERPETUATING GOVERNMENT

Government is mostly made up of people who are incapable of controlling the expenditures of that very same government. I've mentioned the impact of regulation and we'll get back to it throughout this book. Why would the taxpayers allow the waste I'm about to detail? More importantly, why would our current government officials allow this?

The answer is that they are either incompetent or compromised. George W. Bush presided over a massive increase in the national debt in 2004 when Republicans had control of Congress and the Senate did nothing to rein in the waste. Barack Obama presided over an even bigger increase, partly under Democratic control of Congress, partly under Republican control.

This is only a small list. Do you think a board of directors made up of experts and business people, as detailed in the next chapter, would allow this? Hell no! That is why we must elect government officials who are dedicated to spending our tax dollars wisely. Government is too big and out of control. The people who know this unconscionable waste the best are the government's own employees. We should create a program as I propose in Chapter 5, with high dollar rewards for ideas from whistleblowers – government employees who are closest to the waste – on how to cut that excess spending. We should protect these employees from any form of retaliation. I would not be surprised if that initiative alone cut government spending by 5 percent.

Government spending must be cut because the national debt of more than $19 trillion exceeds the annual GDP, our total national output of goods and services, of about $17 trillion. The U.S. is one of the top countries guilty of letting this happen. Japan is another (its debt is about double the size of its economy) and has been mired in stagnation for nearly two decades. An obvious approach to remedying this situation is cutting frivolous government spending. Look at the presidential election and the Presidential Election Campaign Fund, even though voluntary, which contains tens of millions of dollars. As Forbes contributor Doug Bandow asked in a column, "What could be dumber than forcing the American people to pay for the campaigns and conventions of the very politicians who created today's mess?"[9]

Congressman Bill Posey (R-Florida) lists some, but certainly not all, of the worst offenders on his website (www.posey.house.gov):

Dept. of Agriculture: Tighten Controls on Federal Employee Credit Cards and Cut Down on Delinquencies: A recent audit revealed that employees of the Department of Agriculture (USDA) diverted millions of dollars of taxpayer funds for personal purchases through their government-

---

[9] http://www.forbes.com/sites/dougbandow/2012/01/16/nows-the-time-to-start-cutting-wastefulgovernment-programs/#62e578eb2691

issued credit cards. In a sampling of 300 employees' purchases over six months, investigators estimated that 15 percent abused their government credit cards at a cost of $5.8 million. Taxpayer-funded purchases included Ozzy Osbourne concert tickets, tattoos, lingerie, bartender school tuition, car payments and cash advances."[10]

Dept. of Agriculture: Dead, Duplicate, and Disqualified Food Stamp Recipients: The USDA Inspector General found roughly 2,000 dead people are still receiving food stamps in New York and Massachusetts combined. Additionally, its investigation revealed 7,236 people in these states are receiving duplicate benefits, while 286 are on state lists that should exclude them from receiving food stamps. These unnecessary payments amount to $1.4 million every month.[11]

Dept. of Energy: One Billion in Energy Tax Credits for Prisoners and Children: As much as $1 billion or more in tax credits for energy efficient residential improvements are being claimed by individuals with no record of owning a home, including prisoners and underage children.[12]

Dept. of Health and Human Services: Billions in Payments for Tax Cheats: One of the largest federally funded programs, Medicaid, provides billions of dollars in payments to tax cheats who owe millions in unpaid taxes. Almost 7,000 Medicaid providers in just three states owed $791 million in unpaid federal taxes but received $6.6 billion in Medicaid reimbursements in just

---

[10]http://www.heritage.org/research/reports/2010/10/how-to-cut-343-billion-from-the-federalbudget

[11]http://www.coburn.senate.gov/public/index.cfm?a=Files.Serve&File_id=b7b23f66-2d60-4d5a8bc5-8522c7e1a40e

[12]http://www.coburn.senate.gov/public/index.cfm?a=Files.Serve&File_id=b69a6ebd-7ebe-41b7bb03-c25a5e194365

one year according to a Government Accountability Office (GAO) investigation.[13]

Dept. of Defense: Going green for $27 a gallon: The Pentagon paid $12 million for 450,000 gallons of biofuel in order to show off its new "Great Green Fleet" of energy-efficient equipment and operations. However, at nearly $27 a gallon the fleet probably won't be getting very far. The Navy is not the Department of Energy and is not the proper place to fund alternative energy research.[14]

Dept. of Health and Human Services: Medicaid Overpayments: The House Committee on Oversight and Government Reform estimates that New York State overbilled the federal government by $15 billion over the past 20 years for Medicaid costs for developmentally disabled patients, an amount that exceeded the entire Medicaid budgets of 14 states.[15]

It is not just the waste, but also the corruption, that is alarming.

Let's look at another blatant example of corruption paired with wasteful spending: the $1.4 billion taxpayer bailout for Robert Kennedy's "green" company, BrightSource.

Ironically, the loan was issued by a former employee of BrightSource, who, after raising money for Obama's 2008 presidential campaign, became an official at the Department of Energy (DOE) and granted the loan. This is one example of *many*

---

[13]http://www.coburn.senate.gov/public/index.cfm?a=Files.Serve&File_id=b7b23 f66-2d60-4d5a8bc5-8522c7e1a40e

[14] http://www.reuters.com/article/2012/07/02/us-usa-navy-greenfleet-idUSBRE86106X20120702

[15] http://thehill.com/blogs/healthwatch/medicaid/250711-gop-slams-15-billion-in-medicaidoverpayments

investor connections with government, which sooner or later become the U.S. taxpayers' problem. [16]

According to investigative journalist and Breitbart.com editor Peter Schweizer in his book, *Throw Them All Out*, Kennedy netted a $1.4 billion bailout for BrightSource through the loan guarantee issued by the former employee-turned-DOE-official. The details of how BrightSource managed to land its ten-figure taxpayer bailout have yet to fully emerge. But the question could be answered by Sanjay Wagle.

According to an article on Breitbart.com in November 2011, Wagle was one of the principals in Kennedy's firm who raised money for Barack Obama's 2008 presidential campaign. When Obama won the White House, Wagle was installed at the DOE, advising on energy grants.

From an objective vantage point, investing taxpayer monies in BrightSource was a risky proposition at the time. In 2010, BrightSource, whose largest shareholder is Kennedy's VantagePoint Partners, was up to its eyes in $1.8 billion of debt obligations and had lost $71.6 million on its paltry $13.5 million of revenue, according to Breitbart.

Even before BrightSource went to the DOE, the company made it known publicly that its survival hinged on successfully completing the Ivanpah Solar Electrical System, which would become the largest solar plant in the world, on federal lands in California.

What's more, BrightSource touted the Ivanpah project as a green jobs creator. Yet as its own website reveals, the thermal solar plant will only create 1,400 jobs at its peak construction and 650 jobs annually thereafter. Even using the peak estimate of 1,400

---

[16] http://www.freerepublic.com/focus/f-news/2808401/posts

jobs, that works out to a cost to taxpayers of $1 million per job created.

As the *Washington Times* reported in March 2015, Federal agencies across the board are continuing to waste tens of billions of taxpayer dollars on duplicative spending efforts, even after Congress's official watchdog has made hundreds of recommendations for cutting back.

The spending issues, ranging from Medicare and Medicaid mismanagement to transportation programs to weapon systems acquisitions, cost taxpayers $125 billion in improper payments in 2014 alone, the newspaper reported, citing the GAO.

When you Google "government wasteful spending," you get 8,040,000 results.

Do you think any business would tolerate this type of waste? The answer is NO! They have shareholders that they are accountable to. We, the taxpayers own the Federal government and WE are the shareholders. The Federal government treats us like dirt. This must change.

Government workers make 78 percent more than those in the private sector.[17] Average pay and benefits for government employees is $52,688 higher than for non-government employees. That is approximately $140 billion more a year spent on federal employees compared to their counterparts in the private sector ($52,688 x 2,633,000[18]). This is according to the Cato Institute, which bases its findings on figures from the U.S. Bureau of

---

[17] http://freebeacon.com/issues/study-government-workers-make-78-percentmore-than-private-sector/

[18] Number of federal government employees cited by OPM.gov: https://www.opm.gov/policy-data-oversight/data-analysis-documentation/federal-employment-reports/historical-tables/total-government-employment-since-1962/

Economic Analysis. In addition, the study found that Federal government workers earned an average of $84,153 in 2014, compared to an average of $56,350 made in the private sector.[19] When including benefits for federal workers, the difference between government and the private sector increases even more dramatically. Federal employees made $119,934 in total compensation last year, while private sector workers earned $67,246, which equates to the difference of over $52,000, or approximately 78 percent.

Tax dollars are 100 percent generated by the private sector. The taxes raised from the private sector pay for 100 percent of government. To break it down further, government benefits per employee were $35,781 versus private sector benefits of $10,896.

Are the taxpayers crazy for allowing these abuses? The truth is that many of us feel unable to make them stop, though they are committed blatantly and apparently without remorse.

Nearly 70 percent of Americans say they are concerned that public employee unions have too much influence over politicians, who, when elected, must negotiate with these groups. Total union political contributions were $925 million in 2004 and now are $1.7 billion range, according to the Huffington Post (3/15/2014).

Public employee unions should not be allowed to make political contributions. Who represents the hardworking taxpayer? Nobody is helping us. The politicians reward the union employees with high salaries and benefits that do not exist in the private sector. These issues are not Democratic or Republican issues. The real issue is what is fair to the taxpayer.

Why are politicians not regulated but everyone else is? This is why we must rein in our government and make it the government for the *taxpayer* and not for the government employee. Do you

---

[19] IBID

think business executives would overpay for services? The answer is no. That is why, as you'll see in the next chapter, we need a board of directors for each department and agency.

In November 2011, the CBS TV newsmagazine 60 Minutes did a segment on insider trading within Congress. This brought to light the unfair reality that while everyone else is subject to insider trading rules, Congress is exempt. This is difficult to comprehend considering one would imagine Congress has access to non-public information. It wasn't until this was exposed that Congress moved quickly in an effort to regain public trust and passed the STOCK Act in 2012. However, it was secretly modified in April 2013 and key transparency provisions amended, rendering the act effectively useless. [20]

Skepticism rises when the public watches government officials spend millions of dollars campaigning, all in an effort to keep their $174,000 a year jobs. If politicians leave government with more money in their pockets than when they arrived, it is hard not to think it is due to privileged information at their fingertips. "Washington has a long history of self-dealing," according to former Democratic Representative Brian Baird of Washington state. In a 2012 press release Baird says:

"The town is all about people saying – What do you know that I don't know. This is the currency of Washington, D.C. And it's that kind of informational currency that translates into real currency. Maybe it's over drinks, maybe somebody picks up a phone. And says you know just to let you know it's in the bill. Trades happen. Can't trace 'em. If you can trace 'em, it's not illegal. It's a pretty great system. You feel like an idiot to not take advantage of it."

---

[20] http://www.opensecrets.org/news/2013/04/action-alert-stock-act-reversalsigned/

At retirement, House and Senate members collect $174,000 a year for life. This is so unfair for the overburdened taxpayer. The taxpayers must revolt by holding elected officials to a very high standard.

We'll see exactly how in the next chapter.

"We are going to turn the government into something that looks more like a well-run business than a behemoth of inefficiency." – Dr. Ben Carson, 2016 presidential candidate, as quoted in the Washington Post, May 11, 2015

Chapter 4

THE SOLUTION, PART 1: GOVERNMENT BOARDS OF DIRECTORS

Now that you're convinced, and I hope outraged, at how needless regulation and outright fraud have crippled our government and our businesses, let's look at the first part of the solution, which should be fairly easily to understand and to implement, if we can summon the political will. It has two major components, which we'll examine in the next three chapters

The first is creating boards of directors for all Federal departments and agencies so they can be run like businesses, not necessarily to turn a profit, but to cut waste and unnecessary regulations. The second, which we'll look at in detail in Chapter 5, related to this, is providing the needed information to these boards by rewarding rather than punishing whistleblowers throughout the government and society. These are the people on the ground who know that most have too long been discouraged or even jailed when pointing out the absurdities that we've seen in government spending or private business practices.

Government agencies rely on regulation and costly infrastructure to provide services rather than common business sense. If government were a business, it would be out of business. There is no accountability for regulation or its expense. The government should be held accountable for spending our tax dollars efficiently.

Certainly the government has costly responsibilities, including defense and much social spending, but as we've seen, the $2 trillion in annual cost of regulation is a job killer. Let's spend a little more time on figures from that 2014 National Association of Manufacturer's report. NAM concludes that complying with Federal regulations costs all companies about $10,000 a year per employee; manufacturers nearly $20,000 per employee; and manufacturers with fewer than 50 employees a whopping $35,000 per employee per year. In total some $140 billion is spent complying with the rules, and the companies surveyed said that if they had that money they'd plow nearly all of it back into investment. Think of the jobs!

Again, this cost of regulation is equivalent to more than half the amount the government collects on taxes, a burden on companies as well. As the NAM report shows, cutting regulations is the low-hanging fruit – nearly all of it goes straight back into creating jobs.

How do we get started unraveling this mess, with government today reaching into every part of our lives and into every business? It really shouldn't be that hard. To the extent that government departments are organized at all, they aren't organized along any lines a businessperson would recognize. Why not? Well, the best explanation I've ever seen is that they never have been.

That needs to change – immediately. By executive order the next president, who after all is the head of the executive branch, should scrap the present system and start over. Congress would need to authorize funding for these agencies, as it does now, but wouldn't be able to block the new structure, which is the President's prerogative. Every government agency should have a board of directors made up of seasoned business executives and eminent industry experts equally divided between Democrats and Republicans (and as many true independents as we can find) who either volunteer their services or receive modest compensation. These executives can be selected by a group of the leading executive search firms that might volunteer their services or charge modest fees. The first task of the board would be to name a CEO to run the agency, in coordination with the cabinet secretary, appointed by the President, who would act as sort of a Chairman.

These boards would follow the best practices of activist boards whose members use their knowledge and experience to drive management, rather than the practices of docile boards that rubber stamp the decisions of their friends who put them on the board in the first place. Examples of the latter would be Enron, whose board did nothing to detect or prevent one of the worst scandals ever (See Chapter 5) and the current Volkswagen directors who have allowed a scandal over emissions testing to endanger the future of the car maker. Conversely, boards at Microsoft and General Motors have recently moved decisively to appoint new leaders, the first case succeeding the founding group, and in the second case inheriting and fixing a scandal with the potential to derail the company as Volkswagen's has, but which has been handled much more intelligently. In these cases, the boards didn't delay confronting problems, didn't bow to internal factions, and made the right decisions for customers, employees and shareholders. That's exactly what these government boards need to do. Gather the best available information and then act decisively, in the best interests of the country.

But wouldn't it be hard to find such directors? Thomas J. Neff, CEO of Spencer Stuart, one of the largest worldwide executive recruiting firms, thinks not. "I am confident there would be an ample pool of talent willing to serve," he said in an email to the author in February 2016. He added that recently retired executives would be particularly willing and available to serve. Think of the talent. Jack Welch of GE, Philip Condit of Boeing, Sanford Weill of Travelers. The list goes on.

There are also hundreds of thousands of less well-known but highly qualified experts and business veterans who are either retired or out of work, but who would be eager to help their country by helping the government run better. This is a huge pool of untapped, and frankly, frustrated talent that we've squandered for too long. It's the lever that can move the boulder.

Every company has a board of directors that has oversight of the company's activities. The Federal government is really the largest company in the world and needs to be run like one. There is no effective oversight of the government agencies. They provide goods and services just like a business and should be run that way. What we have now is a bunch of politicians with little to no experience supervising all of the government agencies. Look at the mess we are in. We need CHANGE, the right kind of change.

Some of the other objectives of the boards will be as follows:

a. Determine the purpose of every agency in the department and what regulations they control. How can those regulations be improved and streamlined?

b. Are the services of the agency necessary?

c. Are the services being provided in the most cost-effective manner?

d. Can any of the work they provide be outsourced to the private sector on a more cost-effective basis?

e. Is the compensation being paid to the agency employees competitive with the private sector?

f. If the salary and benefits are not competitive, they should be adjusted immediately (either upwards or downwards).

g. Are they using cost-effective technology?

h. Do they have the proper controls in place to prevent fraud and waste?

i. Is there proper accounting, financial and management reporting in place to evaluate the effectiveness of the agency?

Why do I choose business executives for these boards, rather than bureaucrats? Business creates 100 percent of our country's jobs. Government only exists because of the taxes created by business. Without business there would be no government. Does government have too much power? There is no doubt about it.

Why do politicians not work? It is simple. They are compromised because they have raised money from special interest groups. They owe these groups favors and do not make decisions that are best for the country. Congressmen are elected for two years and spend half of that time running for re-election and fundraising.

If businesses were run by part-time executives with no experience they would be out of business. The sad truth about government is that it is like a company facing bankruptcy that needs help fast.

Governor Rick Scott has eliminated 4,000 regulations in the state of Florida. Rick was a successful businessman who was concerned about the way the country was headed and decided to run for governor. He won in 2010 and was re-elected in 2014. He inherited a $3.5 billion deficit. In six years has turned it into a $3.5

billion surplus while improving the quality of life for Floridians. He focused on jobs and education. Florida has created more jobs than any other state over the past six years. The country needs more common-sense businessmen and woman involved in government. In Chapter 2 you read about government waste. If you think business executives would tolerate any waste, you are wrong.

John Kasich, the governor of Ohio who ran for the GOP nomination this year, wrote an interesting Action Plan for streamlining several government agencies.[21] In the section on the Commerce Department he says: "For at least 30 years people have talked about dismantling the 40,000+ employee, $12 billion U.S. Department of Commerce to help shrink the Washington bureaucracy. The reason is simple: The Department has become a cluttered "attic" for the federal government, hiding political pet projects, outdated programs, and agencies without a logical home. The resulting "Franken-agency" simply no longer makes sense. John Kasich will do more than just talk about this monstrosity – as president he will eliminate it, as part of an overall freeze and reduction of the federal workforce. Essential work of Commerce would be transferred to other agencies, and unneeded programs, political projects, and expensive bureaucracy – as well as the cabinet position itself – would be eliminated.

The key is how! Only a board of directors made up of experienced business people can get this done. Politicians have proven themselves to be inept.

Eric Schnurer, writing in the Atlantic in May 2013, offers a thoughtful list of first steps:

---

[21] https://www.johnkasich.com/resultsnow/

"To make government work in the 21st century requires the same basic 'business plan' as in any other failing, but potentially still viable, enterprise:

- First, resize it to current realities – stop the bleeding, cut the fat, and get the existing operation on stable footing. Then, start thinking about the future – or, more accurately, the present that's already arrived while the enterprise remained stuck in the past;

- Redesign the business, its products, services, and organization, to meet current and future demand – you wouldn't keep selling buggy whips if people wanted cars. And then,

- Redefine and reposition the enterprise to compete effectively against new competitors and in whole new markets.

All these are exactly right, and again, it's going to take boards of business people and independent industry experts to make the necessary changes.

Let's take that same Commerce Department that Gov. Kasich wants to eliminate. That may or may not be the right thing to do, since the agency does do work that other agencies would need to pick up, but a board comprised of people like Jeffrey Immelt, CEO of General Electric; Michael Corbat, CEO of Citigroup; John Kotter of Harvard Business School; and Larry Fink of Blackrock could determine that fairly quickly. They could offer a real plan for eliminating each and every wasteful regulation and resizing and refocusing the department in order to help businesses and create jobs.

For the biggest of them all, the Department of Defense, the same logic holds. Let's give real power to a board consisting of the likes of Jack Welch, former CEO of General Electric; Colin

Powell; Mitt Romney; Gen. David Petraeus; efficiency expert Michael Porter of Harvard; and John Chambers of Cisco. They could and would unleash consultants on very short-term contracts to scour every program and budget item and produce brutally honest reports and what's working and what's not. Would such a board put up with $900 hammers and multi-billion-dollar aircraft the Air Force doesn't want? I don't think so. Would Jack Welch, known for firing the bottom 10 percent of his employees each year, tolerate poor performance? I think not.

Imagine if the same thing happened with Education, Health, Interior, State and all the other departments. As detailed in Chapter 2, the Immigration and Naturalization Service of the Department of Homeland Security and the Internal Revenue Service of the Treasury Department are ripe for boards that would strip away needless regulation, free up billions in tax dollars and let in the people we need to grow our economy.

Let's also have a look at the Interior and Transportation Departments, responsible for much of our crumbling infrastructure. Imagine a board consisting of William Ford, Elon Musk of Tesla, and Larry Page of Google, among others, tasked with establishing a priority lists of projects, ideas for funding them, making sure anything road or bridge or tunnel that's rebuilt would be compatible with "smart" or driverless cars and new, high-speed rail ideas. In other words, with this and all the new boards, plan with the future in mind before committing to anything so that newly built infrastructure is both durable and adaptable.

The Interior Department also manages one of our great national treasures, the National Park Service, which millions of us enjoy. But the NPS also manages huge swaths of federally owned land that aren't suitable for recreation, some of which could be developed. Again, a board of directors that is both bi-partisan and expert could make recommendations to Congress and the public free of lobbying interests, and would be credible and effective. Hundreds of billions of dollars would be freed up for infrastructure projects or returned to taxpayers as tax cuts. Thousands of regulations would be repealed or not be renewed, which as we've seen above, would create millions of jobs.

None of these government departments actually manufactures anything, although many buy goods and service from contractors. But, as we've seen, the regulations they produce are strangling American business. With business leaders and union representatives and academic experts working together, public and worker health and safety can be maintained while the really useless rules are cleared away.

Let's also take a look at the Department of Veteran's Affairs, a crucial department for the millions of veterans who've served our country with distinction, often at great personal loss or injury. While many veterans deservedly enjoy first-rate care at VA hospitals, there is still an embarrassing and inexcusable backlog and unacceptable waiting times for treatment at some facilities for far too many veterans.

An article in USA Today (5/27/14) highlights the scope of the veterans' medical network. It is comprised of 9 million patients, 950 facilities and 85 million annual appointments; however its size does not excuse the copious amount of problems associated with the Department of Veterans Affairs, which continues to be cited for waste, and accused of fraud, abuse and theft. Size and complexity is not an excuse to let this slide. It is never an excuse in business.

An article in the *Fiscal Times* from 2015 states that the Veterans' Affairs Secretary, Bob McDonald, himself a successful businessman and turnaround artist before entering the administration, says "his department is so cash-strapped that it's struggling to accommodate the massive number of veterans seeking treatment." Clearly his hands are tied. If he were the head of or member of a board of directors charged with cleaning things up, he could make a lot more progress.

Certainly the federal agency entrusted to stretch tax dollars as far as they can go to get veterans the best medical care is not spending our tax dollars wisely. It's not helping monetarily or, even worse, health-wise.

According to the *Fiscal Times* story, McDonald has urged Capitol Hill to focus on the fact that the VA has 336 buildings across the country, covering about 10.5 million square feet, that are either sitting vacant or less than 50 percent occupied. He has called upon lawmakers to close or consolidate the facilities, but nothing has been done. If this agency were run by a board of directors, testimonies of corruption and waste would hold it accountable to make change. The board would immediately think of closing or consolidating underutilized facilities to free up millions of dollars that could otherwise be used to pay more doctors and nurses to treat the backlog of patients at VA facilities across the country.

Yet, delayed care and falsified records continue to spread, accompanied by heartbreaking tales from veterans and their families.

USA Today reported the following statistics in 2014:

- More than 100,000 veterans are waiting to see doctors.
- In Florida, 8,500 veterans have been waiting more than 3 months for appointments.
- In Phoenix, 58 veterans died while on secret waiting lists.
- A new audit found 64 percent of VA facilities falsified wait times, and 13 percent of schedulers were actually trained to engage in fraud.

- The longest waits are for mental health services. Veterans' suicides, though falsely reported to be low, are at 22 per day or an outrageous 8,030 every year.

U.S. Rep. Jeff Miller of Florida was quoted in the *Washington Times* on Sept. 2, 2015 as saying: "(The VA is) failing and continuing to fail ... The veterans deserve better. The status quo doesn't work. Are you going to stand with the veterans or the bureaucrats? I know where your hearts are – it's with the veterans, and of course it's with the employees and the people. But there are some rotten people that work in the department that need to be fired, not protected."

A board of directors could address this problem immediately and effectively, either placing waiting patients in private or underused government hospitals, or hiring more staff at existing facilities, or both. These backlogs would crush a private business, and they shouldn't be allowed in government.

Here are some possible boards of directors for each cabinet-level department or agency, and some top agenda items for each. This is far from a definitive list and is merely illustrative. I have no idea if a future president would pick them or if they would serve. I'm not endorsing any of them. But you'll notice a diversity of experience and party. There is a huge pool of untapped talent in this country that could be put to work to root out inefficiency, propose sensible business solutions and practices, and slam the door on waste and fraud. There are massive problems in every government agency and department that need to be addressed if we want to unleash our potential and keep our country great. Let's put them to work.

Department of State:

Board:

Thomas Pickering (former U.S. Ambassador to the UN; Nicholas Burns (former Undersecretary of State for Political Affairs; Richard Haass (President, Council on Foreign Relations"; George P. Schultz; Madeline Albright, Condoleeza Rice and James Baker (former Secretaries of State); Anne-Marie Slaughter (former dean of Princeton's Woodrow Wilson School of Public and International Affairs: Joseph Nye (former dean of Harvard's John F. Kennedy School of Government); Kevin Ryan (Gilt Group); George H. W. Bush; Bill Clinton.

Agenda:

Examine the security and effectiveness of our embassies and consulates; reallocation of resources used to communicate America's message abroad; reallocation of foreign aid; modernize global communications. Become leading force for free and fair trade.

Department of the Treasury

Board:

Michael Bloomberg; Larry Kudlow; Steve Forbes; Warren Buffett; Jamie Dimon; William Simon; Jeffrey Sprecher (Intercontinentalexchange); Edward Chaplin (MBIA); Stephen Schwarzman (Blackstone); Lloyd Blankfein (Goldman Sachs); Paul Singer (Elliott Management Corp.); Charles Schwab; Chuck Leek; Kenneth I. Chenault (American Express);

Agenda:

Reexamine borrowing and investing of U.S. funds; audit every agency and office; bring modern technology to IRS. Get rid of those 74,000 pages of regulations!

Department of Defense
Board:

Colin Powell; Jack Welch; Philip Condit; Sanford Weill; Gen. David Petraeus;, Michael Porter (Harvard Business School economist); John Chambers (former CEO of Cisco).

Agenda:

Reexamine all defense procurement spending and make sure all are competitive. (No more $35 billion fighters or $900 hammers!) Reallocate personnel where needed. Upgrade technology at all levels.

Department of Justice
Board:

Derek Bok (Harvard); Sandra Day O'Connor; Rudy Giuliani; Chris Christie; Cory Booker (former Newark, N.J. mayor).

Agenda:

Re-examine criminal justice system top to bottom. Upgrade technology to allow all levels to communicate. Integrate local knowledge and preferences to improve policing, reduce court backlogs and explore sentencing and prison alternatives. Conduct national dialogue on drug enforcement.

Department of the Interior
Board:

Bruce Babbitt (former U.S. Secretary of the Interior and governor of Arizona); Jon Huntsman (former governor of Utah and ambassador to China and Singapore).

Agenda:

Re-examine Federal land ownership to ensure best use of our resources. Improve communications with local landowners and governments to create jointly agreed land development programs. Work with resource companies to find environmentally acceptable solutions to mining and drilling issues.

Department of Agriculture

Board:

Hugh Grant (Monsanto); Gov. Terry Branstad (R-Iowa); Chris Roberts (Cargill); Jimmy Carter; Rick Perry.

Agenda:

Secure a safe food supply while freeing farmers to do their jobs. Eliminate wasteful rules and obsolete subsidies. Reduce paperwork at all levels by upgrading technology.

Department of Commerce

Board:

Carly Fiorina; Jeffrey Immelt (GE); Michael Corbat (Citigroup); John Kotter (Harvard); Laurence Fink (Blackrock); Mark Cuban (owner of the Dallas Mavericks, *Shark Tank*); Marvin Ellison (JCPenney); Mark Andreesen (Silicon Valley entrepreneur): Bill Gates; Steve Case (founder of AOL); Jeff Bezos; John Chambers, Reed Hastings (Netflix); Tim Cook (Apple); Mark Zuckerberg (Facebook); Ginni Rometty (IBM); Meg Whitman (HP); Michael Dell; Martha Stewart; Ursula M. Burns (Xerox).

Agenda:

Become a force for entrepreneurship, manufacturing and services job creation and elimination of needless regulation. Establish task forces in all areas to cut harmful rules and upgrade technology throughout the country. Lead effort to bring best technology to all levels of government.

Department of Labor

Board:

Richard Trumka (president, AFL-CIO); Rosabeth Moss Kanter (Harvard Business School), Mark Benioff (Salesforce.com); Howard Schultz (Starbucks); Terry Lundgren (Macy's); Larry Ellison; Doug McMillon (Wal-Mart); Indra Nooyi (Pepsico); Steve Easterbrook (McDonald's); Craig Jelinek (Costco); Thomas Neff (Spencer-Stuart).

Agenda:

Eliminate harmful regulations that impede small and large businesses and startups from hiring the people they want.

Department of Health and Human Services

Board:

Steven Brill (founder, Court TV, *The American Lawyer*); Dr. Ben Carson; Cecile Richards (President, Planned Parenthood); George Paz (CEO, Express Scripts); David Reich (Mount Sinai); Kenneth C. Frazier (Chairman & CEO, Merck); Joseph Mario Molina MD (CEO, Molina Healthcare)

Agenda:

Remove all regulations that hamper doctors and patients from getting efficient care and the medications they need at world-competitive prices.

Department of Housing and Urban Development

Board:

David Simon (Simon Property Group); Donald Trump Jr. (EVP, The Trump Organization); Sam Zell (Equity Group Investments; Tribune Co.); Oprah Winfrey.

Agenda:

Remove outdated regulations that prevent developers from building more housing and renters from finding reasonable priced apartments. Review mortgage process to get rid of harmful or wasteful rules while insuring soundness of process.

Department of Transportation

Board:

Bill Ford; Elon Musk; Larry Page (Oracle); Wilbur Ross (turnaround investor); Mary Barra (GM); Frederick Smith (Fedex); Phil Condit.

Agenda:

Rebuild highways and bridges by removing red tape. Lead effort to introduce driverless cars, smart highways, up to date air traffic control; high-speed rail where these initiatives improve efficiency and keep the U.S. at forefront of developments.

Department of Energy

Board:

Lee Raymond (former CEO ExxonMobil); Rex Tillerson (former CEO, ExxonMobil); Ralph Nader.

Agenda:

Remove all regulations that hinder, rather than help, use of all sources of energy while protecting the environment.

Department of Education

Board:

Richard Levin (Yale); William Bennett (former Secretary of Education); Rupert Murdoch (Fox Corp.); Michelle Rhee (former Schools Chancellor, Washington, D.C.); John Hennessy (Stanford); Derek Bok (Harvard).

Agenda:

Cut rules that overregulate local control of education while encouraging parental freedom of choice and improved standards at all levels.

Department of Veterans Affairs

Board:

Gen. Ray Ordierno (retired U.S. Army Chief of Staff); U.S. Sen. John McCain.

Agenda:

Reinvent troubled agency by streamlining rules and upgrading technology to eliminate care backlogs and cover all veterans.

Department of Homeland Security

Board:

Jules Kroll (Kroll Inc.); Louis Freeh (former FBI Director); George W. Bush; Michael Chertoff (former U.S. Secretary of Homeland Security).

Agenda:

Streamline rules, upgrade technology, improve inter-agency communication, evaluate all programs (such as the Transportation Safety Administration) for continuing need and effectiveness.

The boards could also help introduce whistleblower programs that reward, rather than punish, anybody who suggests ways to run their office better, eliminate red tape and identify lawbreakers. There should be no stigma attached, and impartial bureaus to evaluate all of these claims privately, so that retaliatory or hurtful charges can be weeded out. But this creates more bureaucracy, you say? A little, but one that cuts waste and red tape effectively.

In the next chapter we'll take a deeper look at waste, fraud and abuse. I'll relate the story of how I became a whistleblower uncovering one of the biggest frauds of them all. I'll argue that encouraging rather than shaming and persecuting whistleblowers is a big part of the solution.

"Because that's where the money is." –
Willie Sutton, on why he robbed banks.

Chapter 5
THE SOLUTION, PART II: UNLEASH THE WHISTLEBLOWERS

A s we've already seen, and the rest of this book will make clear, I'm not against all regulations, just stupid ones that make problems worse instead of solving them. A case in point is my industry, the financial services industry, which in an era of thoughtless and misdirected deregulation that left harmful regulations intact, allowed some of the biggest frauds in history. I know this subject intimately. I helped uncover one of the worst.

Let's look briefly at the 10 biggest financial frauds in recent history, and learn how simple regulation could have prevented them. When we review these frauds and see what caused them, we will find that the politician's solution is to create very expense job-killing regulations and laws to solve the problem. This never works because you cannot regulate the next fraud. No one knows what it is going to be. You are always fighting the last war. The only people who know what is happening are the people involved.

Crooks will always be with us, but we must create a program to reward whistleblowers, insiders who know about, and are repulsed by, what they are seeing in their companies, with generous sums of money and immunity from prosecution. None of the 10 frauds we're going to review was performed by one person alone. Let's take the best known one of all, the Bernie Madoff fraud. There were at least five employees who knew what was going on. Do you think Bernie Madoff would have committed his fraud if he knew any of these five people could receive $5 million to $10 million in rewards and immunity from prosecution? The answer is NO! Whistleblowers should be treated as heroes.

I was perhaps the first major whistle blower in 1980 when I exposed Sentinel Financial Instruments and 15 other firms committing tax fraud against the U.S. government. It was no fun. There were no rewards, I incurred legal expenses and there was no protection except near the end, when I was offered a place in the Federal Witness Protection Program, which I turned down. I'll go into this in detail at the end of this chapter, to show exactly what's wrong with the present system, and how it needs to be reformed.

First, let's briefly review some of the 10 worst corporate accounting scandals of all time[22]: For the full list, I recommend the website www.accounting-degree.org/scandals.

We'll see they had a lot of common elements.

The first great scandal of the new millennium was that of Enron, immortalized in the book *The Smartest Guys in the Room* and elsewhere. This fraud, involving the company that revolutionized electricity trading and nearly de-powered the state of California, was uncovered by internal whistleblower Sherron Watkins in 2001. By the end, the fraud cost shareholders $74 billion. Thousands of employees and investors lost their retirement accounts, many employees lost their jobs, and Enron Field in

---

[22] 10 Worst Corporate Accounting Scandals Ever Recorded ...
Video for 10 worst corporate accounting scandals, begins at minute 1:46.
https://www.youtube.com/watch?v=cASbUIysfww – Jul 7, 2014 – Uploaded by Accountants Like.

Houston became Minute Maid Park. Enron's president, Jeff Skilling, went to jail and former CEO Ken Lay died in 2006 before his sentencing on his 10 counts. The essence of the scandal was fraudulent accounting.

Telecommunications giant Worldcom was taken down in 2002 when internal auditors caught up to nearly $11 billion in inflated assets, undoing high-flying CEO Bernie Ebbers, who was convicted of fraud and conspiracy in 2005 and is currently in federal prison. The fraud led to the collapse of the company, cost 30,000 employees their jobs and created $180 billion in losses for investors.

The next in this litany is Tyco, the New Jersey-based conglomerate run by the well-connected CEO Dennis Kozlowski, famous for using company funds to buy a $30 million apartment with a $6,000 shower curtain, and for using Tyco's money to pay half the bill for a $2 million 40th birthday party for his wife on the island of Sardinia, which among other extravagances featured an ice sculpture of Michelangelo's David urinating. This fraud was not uncovered by whistleblowers, but by the Manhattan District Attorney and the SEC. The fraud involved simply siphoning about $150 million from company accounts, fraudulent stock sales and inflated income of about $500 million. Kozlowski was released from jail in 2014. The company's chief financial officer, Mark Swartz, was also convicted in the scheme and was released on parole in 2013.

But the granddaddy of them all, at least that we know about, was the three-decade fraud pulled off by Bernard L. Madoff investment Securities LLC, a Wall Street investment firm that collapsed in 2008 after Bernie told his sons what was going on and they then told the SEC. Madoff and his staff routinely made up trades and squirreled away investor money, by some estimates up to $64 billion. A classic Ponzi scheme, some early investors were paid from money collected from later investors. Nothing was actually earned from trading because no trades were executed. One of the sons killed himself, and his father is currently serving 150 years in federal prison. Efforts to recover and repay a portion of the funds to defrauded investors are still going on.

Several big frauds didn't have the benefit of whistleblowers. These include the discovery in 1998 that Waste Management had reported nearly $1.7 billion in inflated earnings, and later settled a shareholder class-action suit for $457 million. According to accounting-degree.org the new CEO set up an anonymous employee tip line to report fraud, after the fact. The SEC caught Freddie Mac, the federally backed mortgage company, with $5 billion in earnings misstatements. The company was later reorganized. Fannie Mae, the other government-backed lender, had its own scandal a year later.

Some common elements of these frauds are that employees of the firms involved obviously either knew or suspected that not everything was on the up and up. The brave ones blew the whistle, but many others did not. Some were convicted with their bosses; others have never been charged. In all cases these frauds went on far too long.

If the government or industry had a program in place to reward the whistleblowers generously with $1 million to $10 million, based on the value of the information, and immunity from prosecution, these frauds would either not have been committed or they would have been closed down shortly after they started. Instead, our government regulates through the inadequate and out-of-date Sarbanes-Oxley Act of 2002, which costs billions of dollars a year and discourages a lot of firms from going public. Sarbanes-Oxley didn't prevent any of these frauds that occurred after it was enacted, and will not prevent the next.

The government's reaction to these frauds, over time, was two major laws: Sarbanes-Oxley and Dodd-Frank. Sarbanes-Oxley did virtually nothing to solve the problem. As for Dodd-Frank, all it did was introduce new regulations that prevent some old abuses, such as bankers trading for their own accounts, while leaving the major problems, including insider trading, untouched.

The government did start a whistleblower program in 2011 under the Dodd-Frank law, which I applaud – mostly. But like most government initiatives it isn't very smart and it is very limited. It rewards some but not all whistleblowers at some but not all financial institutions, takes forever, and doesn't apply at all to non-financial companies, which are the overwhelming majority in this country, nor to politicians themselves!

According to the SEC website:

"Assistance and information from a whistleblower who knows of possible securities law violations can be among the most powerful weapons in the law enforcement arsenal of the Securities and Exchange Commission. Through their knowledge of the circumstances and individuals involved, whistleblowers can help the Commission identify possible fraud and other violations much earlier than might otherwise have been possible. That allows the Commission to minimize the harm to investors, better preserve the integrity of the United States' capital markets, and more swiftly hold accountable those responsible for unlawful conduct.

"The Commission is authorized by Congress to provide monetary awards to eligible individuals who come forward with high-quality original information that leads to a Commission enforcement action in which over $1,000,000 in sanctions is ordered. The range for awards is between 10% and 30% of the money collected."

That's all fine, but as usual with the government, there have been many snags, some caused by the Dodd-Frank rules themselves.

According to Rachel Louise Ensign and Jean Eaglesham, writing in *The Wall Street Journal* on March 3, 2016: "Of the 297 whistleblowers who have applied for awards since 2011, about 247 – or roughly 83% – haven't received a decision from the SEC, according to data obtained by *The Wall Street Journal* in response to a public-records request. Some of the award claims have been delayed more than two years.

"The SEC's whistleblower program imposes strict deadlines on claimants; at least six people have been denied an award because they didn't submit their claims in time, according to the agency's website. But there are no such time limits for the agency to respond to award claims.

"The backlog is a potentially serious issue for a highly touted program that has quickly become a cornerstone of the agency's efforts to root out securities fraud, paying awards totaling more than $50 million. Experts worry that long delays, if allowed to persist, could deter future tipsters."

And at the other extreme, other government agencies, as usual totally uncoordinated with each other, have paid out ridiculously high awards that if continued would bankrupt any responsible program and leave no money for the massive numbers of whistleblowers who are out there, if encouraged.

According to an ABC News report by Alan Farnham in September 2012, big winners include "Bradley Birkenfeld, the ex-banker whom the IRS paid a record $104 million for ratting out his former banking bosses who had helped U.S. clients to hide money in Swiss accounts, and Cheryl Eckard, a former employee of drug maker GlaxoSmithKline, who fingered faults in manufacturing at one of Glaxo's plants and was awarded $96 million."

This is an example of government waste. Both of these rewards could have been capped at $10 million and the balance could have been used to hire more staff to process claims more quickly.

While these huge settlements are fortunately rare, they do highlight the general case for rewarding whistleblowers. And within reason, it's very cost-effective. *Forbes* magazine cited in 2013 a report from the Taxpayers Against Fraud Education Fund that found nearly $20 billion was recovered in healthcare fraud cases from 2008 to 2012 that were uncovered by whistleblowers. These included a $3 billion settlement from GlaxoSmithKline in 2012 and a $2.3 billion settlement by Pfizer in 2009. The TAFEF report says that whistleblower cases typically return $20 for every dollar they cost to prosecute. A 20-times return on investment is great for any business, and unheard of in government work. It's high time we taxpayers enjoyed these benefits!

As an example of the cost of not treating whistleblowers appropriately, I offer my own story. As I said previously, I was most likely the biggest whistleblower in history in 1980. It was not a distinction I wanted and happened by chance. At that time whistleblowers were viewed very negatively and there was limited protection.

I was attracted to Sentinel Financial Instruments because of the opportunity to become a 5 percent partner and play a major role in running the company. I had enjoyed a successful career starting out as an auditor for PriceWaterhouse, became a CPA, and at age 26 was the corporate controller of the 10th largest Wall Street firm, Weeden & Co., and left to become CFO of Cantor Fitzgerald before joining Sentinel. Sentinel had grown very rapidly in a short period of time, and I thought it would be an excellent entrepreneurial opportunity. Instead, after I was there two weeks, I became concerned about the company's activities, which involved generating large amounts of paper, or non-existent trades, to generate large tax losses for clients.

Let me explain. There were no physical certificates. The U.S. Treasury had stopped issuing the physical certificates several years before. When we refer to deliveries, we are referring to the book entries done at the Federal Reserve system's computers. The Federal Reserve computer kept track of where the securities were versus where the cash was. Artificial transactions in treasury bills and notes were being conducted without purchasing anything from the treasury. These so-called transactions didn't require having to actually go out and buy anything from the Treasury. A dealer would just put something on his books indicating a purchase of transactions or purchase of some volume with some other party that is also self-reversing in that way. This could be done without transactions actually having to exist or be delivered over the delivery network in the government securities market. It didn't require that treasury securities actually exist. The term "Fantasy Island" was used to describe the trading. It was all made up!

Sentinel was part of a group of 15 to 20 companies that traded U.S. government securities in large volumes to create billions of dollars of tax deductions for wealthy clients, many of whom were celebrities. Among their clients were Norman Lear, Sidney Poitier, Henry Mancini, Erica Jong, Christopher Walken, Frank Langella, Michael Landon, and Andy Warhol. Some of the corporate clients were AT&T, Ashland Oil, Eastern Airlines. Procter & Gamble and U.S. Steel.

Here is how a typical transaction would work. A client who was looking for a $1 million loss would deposit $250,000 in cash into a trading account and sign a note for $750,000. This allegedly put them at risk for $1 million. Trades would be put in their account, and at the end of the year they would receive a statement showing that they lost $1 million dollars trading treasury bills, which were treated as ordinary income for tax purposes and had a tax rate of 70 percent. They would receive a gain of $ 250,000 in treasury notes, which were treated as capital gains and taxed at 28 percent. The client would pay a fee of $50,000 to $100,000 for this service. The client would save $700,000 in taxes for the treasury bill loss and have to pay income tax on $250,000 at 28 percent, or $70,000. The client saved $630,000 less a tax-deductible fee of $50,000 to 100,000. To put it simply, they were selling the U.S. government's money for 5 cents to 10 cents on the dollar.

If they had actually done the physical trades, this would have been complicated but legal. But the costs involved for doing actual trades and the market risk inherent in holding billions of dollars of securities and margin calls would have made this virtually impossible to do.

So what actually happened? Sentinel traders would use the current prices in the market and enter those trades into a system that would produce trade confirmations and monthly customer statements. The catch was that all of the trades were trades in which Sentinel was on the other side. No cash or securities ever changed hands. They were paper trades designed to produce favorable tax results to the clients for a fee. The fee was 5 percent to 10 percent of the tax savings. In other words, they were selling the Federal government's tax revenue on a percentage basis. This was not quite what Bernie Madoff was doing because all of his trades seem to have been made up. He wasn't even trading with himself!

After two weeks at Sentinel I learned about this and went to the CEO, Michael Senft, and told him that I believed that the company was committing tax fraud. He assured me that I was wrong and told me to go speak to the partner at Sentinel's auditors Peat, Marwick and Mitchell, and their law firm, Cadwallader, Wickersham and Taft. I met with a Peat, Marwick partner who told me that I was incorrect that anything was amiss, and that 15 firms were doing the same thing and that there was nothing wrong. They had just completed the audit and were satisfied that Sentinel was complying with the law. I then met with a Cadwallader, Wickersham partner and had a similar conversation. They also assured me that what Sentinel was doing was within the law.

No way! The records of the firm were in a mess and the books were out of balance. It took me about two months to make any sense out of them. When I did I saw that the official reports said the company had capital of approximately $40 million, but I knew Sentinel only had about $2 million on hand. I went back to Senft and told him about the situation. He got very angry. He called in the head trader and I explained to him that the customers owed us $38 million.

The CEO ordered the trader to lose the company $38 million and make the customers $38 million in the next month. That would nominally balance the books, but didn't benefit either the company or its customers. I knew this was wrong – it was fraud – and it was not the way a company runs. I got out of there as quickly as I could. I was fortunate enough to receive an offer from PaineWebber to be their corporate controller and left Sentinel after six months.

Several months after I had left the firm, I became concerned about my own personal reputation, because I felt like I had been at the scene of a crime even though I had nothing to do with it. I decided that I would meet with an attorney to see if I had any legal liability. A friend who was at a major law firm referred me to

Stanley Arkin, one of the best known white-collar criminal attorneys.

I set up a meeting with Stanley and his partner Mark Arisohn and told them the story. They told me that I was nuts and that this could not possibly be happening. Stanley trusted that I was smart but given the weight of my accusations, wanted to check my references and meet the following week. When he circled back, he confirmed that I had discovered what was then the largest tax fraud in the history of United States. Stanley arranged through the Department of the Treasury to have me granted immunity from prosecution.

After that I started to meet with the Treasury agents and other government agencies to inform them as to what was going on. I met with various government officials approximately 12 times, in meetings lasting from three hours to five hours, over the course about six months. We went over everything I had seen or heard and reviewed every document I had in my possession.

Approximately one year later, the firm was raided, five of the employees were arrested and all of the records were seized by the government. A case was brought against them and about a year after that it came to trial.

In the *New York Times* of November 23, 1983, there was an article about my case headlined "TAX-FRAUD CASE BEGAN WITH TIP I.R.S. GOT IN '81." The newspaper explained that Federal agents had received confidential information two years prior, which led to a major investigation that culminated on Monday with the indictment of five men accused of arranging fraudulent tax deductions amounting to $130 million. The article explains that I, acting on the advice of my lawyer, came forward voluntarily and provided the information to the United States Attorney's office.

If only it had actually been so simple.

Many other firms that were involved with Sentinel or that were doing the same illegal trading were being investigated. This was an extremely stressful period for me. If that weren't enough, the threats began to arrive. I had more than 100 calls or hang-ups with messages such as "You are dead," "You are going to die," and worse. I had fire engines come to my home at 3 in the morning saying that they received a call that my house was in flames. I was offered witness protection but I turned it down. I was proud of who I was and did not want to go into hiding. I took the train to work and parked at the railroad station, but every night when I returned to my vehicle, I would check underneath it for bombs. On the train people who recognized me would move away and sit elsewhere. The government insisted that my testimony be video recorded in the event I was killed before the trial. It was unsettling, and I was concerned about my family, but it is in my nature to always do the right thing.

Then the trial came and it turned out that I was the government's star witness. I gave my testimony for four days of the eight-day trial. All the defendants had been ordered by their lawyers to stare at me the entire time in an effort to rattle me. (Fortunately the facts were the facts.) It was an intense four days and the cross examination was brutal. I got through it relatively unscathed. The government was very satisfied with my testimony. However, I vividly remember that I did not sleep particularly well during that period. At the end of the eighth day the jury found four of the Sentinel employees guilty, and Michael Senft was sentenced to fifteen years in jail.

Unfortunately It was not over, because there were other companies to go after and I would be called in to help. It was a great relief to learn that I did not have to testify again. In 1985 Edward Markowitz, a Washington-based trader, pleaded guilty to selling $445 million in phony tax deductions. Some of his clients were also famous stars, including Woody Allen, Dick Cavett and Bill Murray. Prosecutor Rudolph Giuliani, later mayor of New York, said that including interest and fines the government stood to recover "a quarter of a billion in tax revenues."

In 1987 Charles Agee Atkins, the celebrated "boy wonder of tax shelters" was accused, along with two of his associates, of engineering one of the largest tax fraud schemes in history. They had created $1.4 billion in false tax deductions (at a 70 percent tax rate that cost the government $980 million in tax revenue). They were convicted in 1987. Atkins's firm, The Securities Group, once held positions in government securities worth $21 billion. The once mighty had fallen.

Why am I telling this painful story? I want to illustrate that frauds are extremely complex and that often only the insiders have any idea the fraud is going on. I am very proud that I prevented many billions of dollars from being lost by the U.S. government, which is directly related to my being brave enough to come forward. The government should be encouraging people to speak up when they see that wrongdoings are occurring in their places of business, and protect them at all costs from prosecution, as well as compensating them with generous financial rewards.

I personally lost hundreds of thousands of dollars in compensation because my new employer was disturbed that I was a government informant. It nearly cost me my job and hurt my advancement at the firm. It also prevented me from seeking other employment because my reputation was tarnished. I was fortunate to use my talents to create the world's most sophisticated equity trading system, which resulted in making that firm a lot of money and helping my career. I'll talk about this system, called COLT, more in Chapter 9. If it was not for that my career could have been permanently damaged by the fact that I found it necessary to tell the truth.

It is interesting to note that this happened in 1981, yet it took our government officials 25 years to enact a whistleblower program. How many billions were lost because of this?

What is wrong with our politicians? They do not think of the government as a business!

Just to give you one example, in 1999 I made $10 million in compensation and our tax advisors Ernst & Young approached me and said they had a tax shelter that could save me millions. Their fee would be 5 percent of the tax saving and the firm performing the work would get 10 percent of the savings. My curiosity was aroused and I went to a meeting with the firm and was appalled to discover that they were doing what Sentinel had done, the only difference being that they were using commodities. I listened carefully to what they were offering and politely turned down their offer. They indicated they were creating hundreds of millions in losses for clients. They were selling the government's tax revenues for 15 cents on the dollar.

I did not want to go to the government again because it would only cost me time and money. The government did not treat me very nicely nearly 20 years before and I could only assume that nothing had changed. Can you imagine if a board of directors in 1983 had heard that the government collected over a billion dollars because of an informant? They most certainly would have jumped on it and established a program that would reward those who came forward with information that was so beneficial to our country. Politicians like regulation. Business people want results.

Erika Kelton wrote an article in *Forbes* in March 2012 that sums up the problems with the existing whistleblower programs. They need to be expanded and completely overhauled.

"Whistleblowers are responsible for some of the federal government's biggest recoveries in fraud cases," she wrote. "The Obama administration recently trumpeted that more than $21 billion has been recovered as a result of whistleblower cases under the False Claims Act – and that total doesn't include the many billions more recovered as a result of criminal fines related to those civil cases. Nor does it include the tens of billions saved by the powerful deterrent effect of that robust whistleblower program."

She went on to document the IRS's reluctance to collect billions of tax revenue from scofflaws with the help of whistleblowers. She asks why the IRS refuses to collect even this low-hanging fruit. Clearly the government needs the money, and this is an easy opportunity.

Kelton writes that Congress decided it would be a good idea to encourage whistleblowers to inform the IRS about significant tax fraud and other tax law violations by offering them a reward from the recoveries. It passed the False Claims Act in December 2006. In the first five years only one new whistleblower was rewarded under the program. The IRS is still sitting on a mountain of whistleblower claims.

"The problem with the IRS whistleblower program isn't the 2006 law or the quality of whistleblower information that the IRS is receiving. The IRS whistleblower office reports that it has received dozens of whistleblower submissions concerning matters involving tax losses greater than $100 million and thousands involving payments that exceed $2 million."

Can you imagine a board of directors sitting in a meeting knowing there were dozens of sales orders in excess of $100 million each and thousands of orders in excess of $ 2 million each that weren't being followed up? They would be on the sales team so fast to get them moving, and give them the resources they needed to make the sales.

Kelton adds: "The real problem lies in the culture of the IRS itself and institutional resistance to whistleblowers." The IRS is screwing the honest taxpayer by refusing to do their job. In a business environment they would all be fired. She writes: "The anti-whistleblower attitude was succinctly expressed by former IRS Chief Counsel Donald Korb shortly after he left the IRS to join a white collar law firm where he defends companies against the IRS. In a 2010 interview with the publication *Tax Notes* he said: 'The new whistleblower provisions Congress enacted a couple of years ago have the potential to be a real disaster for the tax system. I believe that is it is unseemly in this country to encourage people to turn in their neighbors and employers to the IRS as contemplated by this particular program. The IRS didn't ask for these rules. They were forced upon it by Congress.'"

Given that thinking, it is no wonder that the IRS fails to collect hundreds of billions of dollars a year. It is a disgrace to the honest tax-paying public that the IRS is able to decide what laws it wants to enforce. If you think that a board of directors would put up with that type of crap you are sadly mistaken. The IRS fails to collect about $300 billion every year. You may have wondered why, when I stumbled upon another tax fraud against the U.S. government, that I failed to report it. I think you know the reason now.

"It is time for our regulators to work with practitioners to develop solutions that are in the best interest of the marketplace. Remember you are tampering with the most efficient capital raising and job creating mechanism in the world – The NASDAQ STOCK MARKET. I look forward to your response."[23] – Letter from the author to the SEC.

Chapter 6

A DEEP DIVE INTO THE WORST JOB-KILLING REGULATION OF ALL TIME

A report issued by consultants Grant Thornton in 2012 concluded that Arthur Levitt, former head of the SEC, through reckless regulation in 1997 caused the United States to lose 18 million jobs over the following 15 years. Grant Thornton's report, "An Instinct For Growth," confirms what I, co-founder of the world's largest marker maker, wrote 18 years ago. On February 4th 1997, I sent a letter to Alfred R. Berkley, the president of the NASDAQ, Arthur Levitt, Chairman of the SEC; Richard Lindsey, SEC Director of Market Regulation; Mary Shapiro, president of NASDAQ Regulation; and Richard Ketchum, General Counsel NASDAQ, warning them of the negative impacts of proposed (ATS) Automatic Trading System rules. My final remark was the warning that opens this chapter.

---

[23] Walter Raquet's letters to SEC.

I received no response from any of the five. I believe the NASDAQ officials were intimidated by Levitt and Lindsey was his enforcer. Arthur Levitt was so out of touch with reality and was on a mission to punish NASDAQ and its market makers to such an extent that he overlooked the big picture...The benefits of the NASDAQ marketplace on our economy.

Levitt did not heed my warnings and pushed through the radical ATS rules which allowed narrower spreads on trades. These narrower spreads so negatively impacted smaller and medium market makers that over time most of them were out of business. The market makers' profits, needed to support research and investment banking for small- and medium-sized companies, no longer existed. Levitt's rules put 450 market-making firms out of business; these firms had handled the majority of small IPOs. Thus, the ATS rules had the unintended consequence of hurting capital formation by driving the smaller dealers out of business. The number of listed companies on the NASDAQ Stock Market went from a high of 8,800 in 1997 to a low of 4,900 in 2012[24]. The regulators threw the baby out with the bath water in their attempt to cure what they believed was too-wide spreads on stocks trading on the NASDAQ. ATS regulations have had a chilling effect on the capital formation process. In addition, ATS rules had the unintended consequences of fostering a market for speculators and day traders.

The SEC could have exempted the small- and medium-size companies from these regulations and preserved the American IPO job-creating machine. Small and medium equities make up 6.6 percent[25] of the market value and a small amount of the trading volume, but represent 81.1 percent[26] of the companies on

---

[24] Grant Thornton Report
[25] Grant Thornton Report
[26] Grant Thornton Report

the exchange. Intel was a $6.8[27] million dollar IPO in the 1970s that now employees 106,000 people.[28] How many Intels did Arthur Levitt kill? The U.S. only does 100 small and medium IPOs per year and now ranks 11th in the world. Thank you, Arthur Levitt!

Bad regulation never stops hurting the economy. We must make government officials responsible for their mistakes. Arthur Levitt was the chairman of the American Stock Exchange from 1978-1989, and then served as SEC chairman from 1993-2001. The Amex, which competed against NASDAQ, languished during his leadership while NASDAQ grew rapidly. I believe Levitt was jealous of NASDAQ's success and, due to his mediocre performance at the AMEX, when he became head of the SEC he decided to get revenge. This led to one of history's greatest examples of bad, devastating, and ill-conceived regulation.

Let's go through the highlights of the Grant Thornton 2012 study to show the damage done.

To start, we have to understand the seemingly arcane subject of "tick size," which just means the smallest unit by which a stock can move. For most of the lifetimes of most U.S. stock exchanges, this was 1/8 of a point, or 12.5 cents. That changed to one penny spreads, and the authors contend that this, applied to less-visible

---

[27]Intel is founded, July 18, 1968 – EDN Community, www.edn.com – July 18, 2015 – Intel was founded on July 18, 1968, by semiconductor pioneers Robert Noyce and Gordon Moore who left Fairchild Semiconductor to do so.

[28]Intel layoffs: Employees say chipmaker changed the rules ... http://www.oregonlive.com/silicon-forest/index.ssf/2015/08/intel_layoffs_former_employees.html Aug. 8, 2015 - "Then it altered the way it selects workers for job cuts, moving away from the way it had handled previous layoffs. The cuts fell disproportionately on older workers too, and a newly applied rule bars laid-off workers from ever being rehired. ... Intel notified laid-off employees (in) June ..."

and less-liquid stocks – the natural state of most public companies and nearly all small public companies – is at the root of the systemic decline in the U.S. IPO market.

It's important because it contributes to trading behaviors that undermine investor confidence. While the current system may be tolerable (trading behaviors aside) for large capitalization and mid-cap stocks with adequate natural liquidity and visibility, it is detrimental to issuers and investors in the more than 80 percent of listed companies that are small-cap and smaller, and do not enjoy natural liquidity and visibility. In other words, it hurts job creators and innovators the most.

Grant Thornton offers quantitative and qualitative evidence that the majority of harm to the U.S. IPO market was caused in 1997 and 1998 by the implementation of the Order Handling Rules and Regulation Alternative Trading Systems, which caused the bankable spread[29] available to small investment banks to drop from 25 cents per share to the minimum tick sizes of 6.25 cents (for NASDAQ stocks priced greater than $10) and 3.125 cents (for NASDAQ stocks priced under $10).

This shift, from a quote-driven to an electronic-order-driven market, set the conditions under which decimalization would be implemented in 2001. However, decimalization, which further eroded the bankable spread from 6.25 cents and 3.125 cents to 1 cent, was a comparatively minor change – essentially a *coup de grâce* that removed any remaining economic incentives required to sustain a vibrant market and help support the U.S. economy.

---

[29] This is a notion that the authors use to describe how spreads are seen from the vantage point of market makers. It is the portion of a spread that market makers can reasonably rely upon to compensate them for their investment in capital, research and sales support. In a quote-driven market (pre-1998), bankable spreads were largely equivalent to quoted spreads, while in the electronic-order-driven market (post-1998), bankable spreads fell to the minimum tick size.

Imagine a stock market in which the cost to buy and sell stocks is "free." While it might appear to be a bright, shiny goal (and the height of deregulation) at first, the reality is that such a market would not survive. There would be no money to pay for research, so research would disappear. There would be no money to pay for salespeople, so all marketing of public company shares would cease. There would be no money to support liquidity, so institutional investors would abandon small companies – which are innately illiquid – in favor of large companies. There would be no money to pay for stock exchanges and alternative trading systems (ATSs). And there would be insufficient standing infrastructure to take companies public, so investor returns would evaporate. The stock market would collapse.

> "The financial system has been wounded by a flood of so-called innovations that merely promote hyper-rapid trading. ...Individual investors are being shortchanged."
>
> John C. Bogle, founder of VANGUARD
>
> "A Mutual Fund Master, Too Worried to Rest" – Jeff Sommer, *The New York Times*, Aug. 11, 2012

The reality today, however, is not far from the above fiction. The U.S. stock market, especially for smaller capitalization companies, has been in a state of progressive erosion that dates back to Regulation ATS and the collapse of tick sizes that culminated with decimalization in 2001 and the implementation of Regulation NMS (the national market system) beginning in 2006. The stock market is in its 15th year of a slow, relentless collapse in terms of numbers of listings, a world where companies delist at a rate three times that at which new companies go public.

Today's stock market is nearly transaction cost-free and overrun by electronic trading schemes that displace investors: Tick sizes are down to a penny or less, and retail commissions are down to $5 a trade. High-quality sell-side research has eroded, as talented analysts have fled Wall Street for hedge funds in what a former head of the Securities Industry and Financial Markets Association's (SIFMA) research committee aptly called the "brain drain." The median market value of companies covered by equity research analysts has steadily increased. There are far fewer investment banks acting as book runners on IPOs than in the 1990s. Middle-market institutional sales desks have all been

Exhibit 1: The "one-two punch" of small tick sizes and the shift to electronic-order-book markets precipitated a secular decline in the U.S. stock markets

Tick size changes on the NASDAQ Stock Market overlaid on the drop in the number of small IPOs

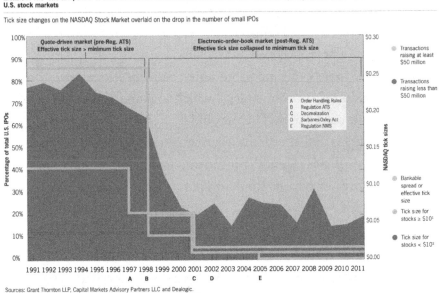

Sources: Grant Thornton LLP, Capital Markets Advisory Partners LLC and Dealogic.
Includes corporate IPOs as of Dec. 31, 2011, excluding funds, REITs, SPACs and LPs.
¹1991: $0.125 for NASDAQ stocks ≥ $10; 1997: $0.0625 for NASDAQ stocks ≥ $10.
²1991: $0.03125 for NASDAQ stocks < $10.

closed. Most of those shouting traders on the floor of the New York Stock Exchange have vanished, replaced by server farms in New Jersey.

Compare this to the period beginning in 1998, when bankable spreads and tick sizes converged in the wake of new Order

Handling Rules and Regulation ATS. The rapid proliferation of electronically posted orders from electronic communication networks (ECNs), crossing networks and other ATSs inexorably drove down tick sizes and bankable spreads to only 1 cent per share – a level that was grossly insufficient to sustain small company capital formation. The aftermarket support model that had worked so well for so long had collapsed, and with it, inevitably, so did small company IPOs.

Starting in 1997, a series of SEC-implemented regulations altered the economic infrastructure on which small companies relied:

Order Handling Rules (1997) required dealers to provide investors with their most competitive quotes. It laid the groundwork for greater competition between dealers, which allowed tick sizes and liquidity to narrow, with new regulations enacted in 1998 and 2001.

Regulation ATS (alternative trading systems) (1998) allowed approved electronic networks to link their securities and orders with registered exchanges. It exposed traditional trading venues like NASDAQ to fierce competition by driving down the volume of orders and reducing tick sizes to 3.125 cents.

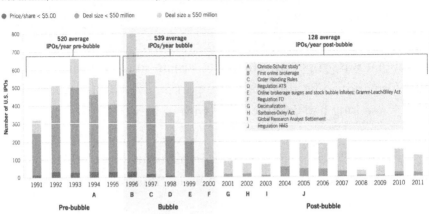

Exhibit 2: The U.S. IPO market is broken

In the last decade, the number of IPOs has fallen dramatically, specifically deals less than $50 million in proceeds

As of year-end 2011, the number of publicly listed companies in the United States had declined 43.5 percent since the peak in 1997. The U.S. stock markets require nearly 388 IPOs a year to replace what is delisted every year. But in fact, there have been an average of 128 IPOs per year since the dot-com bubble burst in 2000. If we excise the post-bubble period of 2000 to 2003 to normalize the data, the market from 2004 through 2011 would require 288 IPOs a year to replace what is delisted every year, versus the actual number of only 146 IPOs per year.

The U.S. stock markets should be producing between 500 and 1,000 IPOs per year. In Grant Thornton's view, stock market structure modifications, beginning with the Order Handling Rules and Regulation ATS, have cost Americans millions of jobs (by depriving companies of public and private capital), depressed economic growth and placed a drag on investment returns (which track economic growth).

Exhibit 4: The U.S. listed markets – unlike other developed markets – have been in steady decline, with no rebound, since 1997

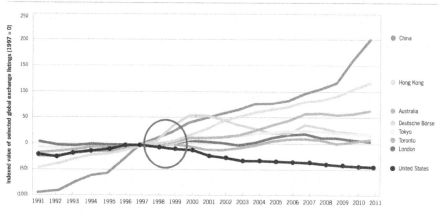

Sources: Grant Thornton LLP, Capital Markets Advisory Partners LLC and World Federation of Exchanges.
Based on the number of listed companies at year-end; excluding funds.
Data as of Dec. 31, 2011.

As a result of this steady erosion in resources committed to capital formation and aftermarket support, the ability of U.S. markets to originate and support new listings is well below the replacement levels needed to support economic growth. The total number of U.S.-listed companies has shrunk every year since 1997 – down 43.5 percent through year-end 2011 – exceeding the number of new IPOs joining U.S. exchanges (see Exhibit 5).

Exhibit 5: The decline in U.S. listings

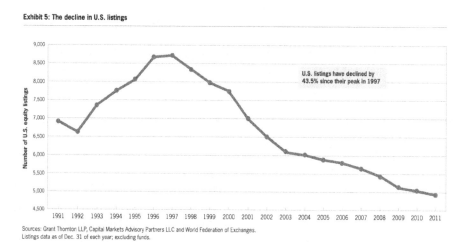

Sources: Grant Thornton LLP, Capital Markets Advisory Partners LLC and World Federation of Exchanges.
Listings data as of Dec. 31 of each year; excluding funds.

[16] www.sec.gov/news/speech/spch509.htm.
[17] An excerpt from an April 10, 2010, letter from Chris Nagy, the head of order strategy and co-head of government relations at TD Ameritrade, to the SEC. Nagy's comments, made in response to the SEC's concept release on market structure, foreshadowed the flash crash, which occurred just one month after his letter.

As mentioned, while 388 new listings per year are needed to maintain a steady number of listed companies, the United States has averaged only 128 IPOs per year since 2001 (see Exhibit 2).[30]

This has resulted in the following:

- **Lower growth:** Efficient markets need to do more than create rock-bottom trading costs for market speculators. Such nearsighted actions, while attempting to alleviate stress for one constituency, have served to destroy the economics for the entire ecosystem. Markets also need to improve the allocation of capital and enhance long-term economic growth. U.S. economic growth will continue to be inhibited by inefficient stock pricing discovery due to the degradation of small company research, marketing support and capital (liquidity) provisions.

- **Job loss:** In today's stock market structure, most small companies' exit strategies no longer include a public listing, but rather a merger or acquisition. When these companies cannot raise capital effectively through the IPO market, they must look to a merger or acquisition, and jobs are lost, not gained. This represents an opportunity cost of millions of jobs and untapped economic growth. We estimate that this loss of IPOs has cost the United States as many as 9.4 million additional jobs that might have been created after companies go public. If we add the private market effect (our best estimate of the multiplier effect in the private market when more companies go public), the number of additional jobs increases to 18.8 million (see Exhibit 6).

---

[30] If we excise the post-dot-com bubble period of 2000 to 2003 to normalize the data, the market from 2004 through 2011 would require 288 IPOs a year to replace what is delisted each year versus the current number of only 146 IPOs per year.

While this is a sorry chapter in over-regulation, it can and should be reversed.

Exhibit 6: A major contributor to employment

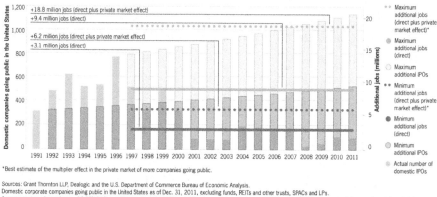

*Best estimate of the multiplier effect in the private market of more companies going public.

Sources: Grant Thornton LLP, Dealogic and the U.S. Department of Commerce Bureau of Economic Analysis.
Domestic corporate companies going public in the United States as of Dec. 31, 2011, excluding funds, REITs and other trusts, SPACs and LPs.
Assumes an annual growth rate of 2.57% (U.S. real GDP growth, 1991-2011) and 822 jobs created on average post-IPO (see "Post-IPO Employment and Revenue Growth for U.S. IPOs," Kauffman Foundation, May 2012).

[18] If we excise the post-dot-com bubble period of 2000 to 2003 to normalize the data, the market from 2004 through 2011 would require 288 IPOs a year to replace what is delisted each year versus the current number of only 146 IPOs per year.

Will Arthur Levitt ever stop? On September 28, 2015, he wrote an article[31] in which he attacked lawmakers who attack regulators. "When was the last time you saw the Financial Services Committee stand up for investor initiatives?" he asked an audience at the annual meeting of the North American Securities Administrators Association, a network of state regulators. He said he could not recall another time in history when securities regulation was more under attack. How many more jobs does Arthur Levitt want to destroy? He should be held accountable for the 18 million jobs he lost for the U.S. and for the economic pain he caused to the middle class.

---

[31] Securities Docket News Wire for September 28, 2015
http://www.securitiesdocket.com/2015/09/29/arthur-levitt-former-sec-chief-blasts-lawmakers-who-attack-regulators-thestreet/

"Once we rid ourselves of traditional thinking we can get on with creating the future." – James Bertrand as quoted on website Leading Thoughts

Chapter 7

DEEP DIVE II: KNIGHT FINANCIAL

As we've seen in the last chapter, out-of-control regulation at the NASDAQ cost us 18 million jobs both directly and in lost IPO start-ups. I consider myself an expert on this because those regulations – specifically the ones requiring decimalization of stock trading – directly harmed one of the fastest-growing companies of all time, the one I co-founded.

In this chapter we'll take a closer look at the startup of Knight Trimark, later Knight Financial, in order to show what was possible before unnecessary regulation stifled innovation in this country. This story simply couldn't happen today. Regulations now don't allow what we did back then; they are completely overwhelming to an entrepreneur. But it could happen again in the future if the board of directors of the SEC repealed those harmful regulations.

In 1993 I was executive vice president of Spear, Leeds and Kellogg, a Wall Street market maker, that took the opposite side of trades for customers – if they wanted to buy we sold, and vice versa – which has since been acquired by Goldman Sachs. Knowing how to manage the risk inherent in such deals was what made us successful. I was in charge of their systems and marketing, but toward the end of the year I looked around and saw opportunities to totally shake up the existing system, which badly needed a shake-up. Incumbent firms were making lots of money the way they always had, but weren't adapting to a changing market or the needs of their customers. I was making a lot of money, more than $1 million a year, but I wanted to create something. I began searching for a niche where I could make a lot more money, and in the words of the currently running GE TV commercial, "change the world.".

In October 1993 I had lunch with Larry Waterhouse, founder of Waterhouse Securities. I had known Larry for many years. We discussed his concern that his competitor Charles Schwab had just acquired an over-the-counter market-making firm. Waterhouse was worried that now that Schwab, which had been one of the first brokers to offer deeply discounted stock trading to the general public, would be able to offer superior execution while making significant profits and put him at a competitive disadvantage. Larry asked if there were any OTC market-making firms that he could acquire. I replied that the larger firms were too expensive and the smaller ones would not be able to provide the quality of trade execution that he would demand. I also said his organization was too small to benefit from the type of transaction that Charles Schwab had just completed. We finished our pleasant lunch, shook hands, and went our separate ways.

That night I woke up at 3 a.m. and had the idea that if I could put five Waterhouse-sized firms together I could create a great company. I hopped out of bed and put together a business plan until 6 a.m. Impatient for the sun to rise, I called Larry at 6:30 a.m., the time I knew he usually arrived for work. I made an appointment for 5 that evening. I did most of the talking, laying out my overnight thoughts. I walked out of his office at 5:45 with a commitment for five million dollars.

Now the work began. How could I put together a first-class market-making company that would challenge the Schwabs of the world? The business plan that I conceived and put together at 3 a.m. never changed. The idea was that management would own 40 percent and the broker-dealer partners together would own 60 percent and control the board of directors. The structure of the broker-dealer share was unique. Half of the profits were based on capital contributed and half on the amount of order flow they gave us. I strongly believed that this would be the fairest method, since order flow is how we would make money. Everyone thought it was a fair formula except one potential investor who wanted a special deal. He argued with me for weeks and we met for dinner and I explained that the partnership was built on trust, and that if I made any exception my integrity would be compromised. He decided not to invest but was a great customer. We kept the offering open for a period of time and I would send him an email every month that would say: Joe, if you had invested $125,000 in Knight I would be sending you a check for $100,000 this month based on your order flow. After a few months he called my partner and begged me to stop sending him the emails.

My next step was to call Ken Pasternak, who was head of trading at Troster Singer, a division of Spear, Leeds where I still worked. Ken was a brilliant trader, and we enjoyed a great relationship. I had taken him on several marketing trips with me. Together we were the perfect combination, I had the technical, marketing and management skills and knew most of the CEOs of the broker-dealers from my previous work. Ken was one of the best traders on Wall Street. I called Ken and explained my idea to him and in less than 10 minutes he said "Let's do it."

Then I started lining up the partners. Ken and I realized that the Internet would change the way trades would be executed and our new company had to be the most technologically advanced market-making firm out there or we wouldn't offer any added value. I realized that small brokerage firms were not big enough to be market makers, and that the firms that had market-making businesses had a distinct advantage. We were going to be the solution to that problem for any of them willing to join us.

Trimark was our first partner, it would make our company, which we were calling Knight, more appealing since through Trimark we could we could perform both NYSE and NASDAQ executions, in addition to OTC trades.

Trimark was one of my customers at Spear, Leeds & Kellogg and I had a great relationship with the principals, Steve Steinman and Rob Lazarowitz. Trimark was also a market maker in competition with the New York Stock Exchange. It was the second largest so-called third-market firm at the time, with a market share of between 1 percent and 2 percent of total NYSE market volume. Ken and I convinced the principals to let Knight acquire the firm for no money down and a 20 percent minority interest in the new firm. Trimark's leadership strongly believed that owning 20 percent of the new entity would be more valuable than their current firm.

Once Trimark was on board, Gruntal & Co. invested $2 million. Gruntal was very interested in investing since it would be clearing the business for Knight, which was very lucrative. Southwest Securities threw in $3 million. Don Buchholz, the CEO, and I had a very long relationship. Joe Ricketts, CEO of Ameritrade was a friend with whom I had done business for many years. He committed $3 million in less than one day. Even more quickly, Scottrade CEO Rodger Riney gave me a $1 million check in fifteen minutes. Even more impressive, to me at least, was

E*TRADE, a tiny company in 1994 with about $1.3 million in capital. But CEO Bill Porter made a big bet and gave us $500,000 to come on board.

All of these commitments and the start-up cash was great, but we wanted to run with as little overhead as possible, so instead of Manhattan we located our office in the then fairly new Harborside project in Jersey City, where rents were considerably cheaper. We were directly across the Hudson from Wall St., linked by ferry boat across the river or PATH train under it. It was a little lonely over there back then, but we were able to lease a 23,000 square-foot floor in a first-class building for $15 per square foot, half of what it would have cost across the river.

In our first temporary space, we were using folding card tables somebody had picked up for $39 as desks, and metal chairs that cost $15. We wanted our employees and partners and clients to understand that we were not into lavish offices and spending foolishly. Our sole mission was to provide superior trade executions to our partners and customers. Our employees quickly got the message, and embraced our culture.

In June 1994 I finally quit my million-dollar-a-year job at Spear, Leeds. Larry Waterhouse gave me a small office and I started to lay out all of the plans and continued fundraising. Three months later Ken Pasternak quit his multi-million-a-year job and began working with me full time. By November we had raised $17 million and were set to go.

After scheduling a celebration party, we received a call informing us that the NYSE was going to forbid any NYSE member from investing in Knight because they felt we were a competitive threat to the exchange. They used an old rule that prohibited a member of the NYSE from owning more than 24.99 percent of a third-market company like Trimark. Tom James,

CEO of Raymond James, dropped out of Knight as a partner because of the NYSE pressure. We were disappointed he didn't join us. About five years later, I had dinner with Tom and his wife. He told me that he made two big mistakes in his life. Number one was that he could have bought the Tampa Bay Buccaneers for $30 million, but instead spent $40 million for the naming rights of the Raymond James Stadium in Tampa. Number two was that he could have invested $5 million in Knight that would later have been worth $400 million.

Richard Grasso, then head of the NYSE, attempted to prevent Knight partners from investing. None of the partners would own more than 9 percent of the partnership, but the NYSE insisted that the broker-dealers were acting in concert and together they owned 40 percent of the new entity. I enlisted Harvey Pitt, managing Partner at Fried, Frank, who would later become the chairman of the SEC, to present our case. We had to give him a retainer of $250,000, which was the last of Knight's money. He spent two and a half months researching and preparing.

Ken, Harvey Pitt and I met Grasso at the NYSE, and Harvey spoke for 40 minutes with no notes. He reminded Grasso and their legal counsel that the NYSE was a monopoly and they were preventing competition. He said that he and his partners were so outraged that they were willing to take this case all the way to the Supreme Court on a contingency basis. His firm was committed to break apart the NYSE monopoly unless we were allowed to go into business. The NYSE had no other option but to give in. Grasso put his hands in the air and said, "I surrender, I'll let the boys go into business."

By February 1995 we had gotten past the life-threatening NYSE and completed the closing documents and funding. It was a very exciting moment in our history, but now the work began. While we had been waiting for the NYSE matter to get settled, we selected office space and put plans together for a 100-person trading room and a large computer facility. We signed the lease in March 1995 and started trading on July 24th of that year. We did some unique things, in line with our initial card table purchases. Trading desks typically cost about $5,000 apiece, which we thought was too high, so we hired a kitchen cabinet maker and our very functional desks cost $1,000. Using the savings on furniture, we spent heavily on technology because we knew we had to have the best. We used a service bureau's system called BRASS, but ran it in-house. This way we could control our own destiny.

We hired a total of 60 employees by opening day. We knew all of the experienced traders on Wall St., but needed trainees, so we put an ad in the New York Times for our training program and received more than 500 resumes. We brought 50 candidates in for interview, and from these hired 10 as full-time employees. We used a test that I came across when I was at Weeden & Co. The test judged the candidates' ability to answer a wide range of questions quickly. I had used this test very successfully at Herzog, Heine, Geduld. Buzzy Geduld was so impressed with the quality of the trainees I was hiring he asked me how I did it. I told him about the test and he made all of the senior traders take it. The results were amazing – with one exception our best traders scored the highest.

In yet another example of how regulations can be perversely applied and interpreted, I got a call the week before we were planning on opening for business from NASDAQ, saying that they had decided that because we were planning on making markets in 2,000 stocks, a special restriction has been placed on $10 million of our capital. This would result in us being unable to meet our minimum capital requirements. We found out that the NASDAQ committee that made the decision was full of our competitors. I knew a lot of top people at NASDAQ, and threatened to sue them for letting this policy go through. Two days later the restrictions were lifted, and we were able to conduct business.

I'm going to quote at length from a speech I gave to all employees at 7 a.m. on opening day, July 24, 1994. I'm doing so because it's a contemporaneous account and shows how close my predictions came to being right. Well, actually I was wrong. A lot of the stuff I said would take two years to accomplish we got done in 18 months.

Ladies and gentlemen:

We are here today because of TRUST.

Our largest customers have entrusted us with $20 million in capital and the orders from their valued customers. They believe we will provide superior execution service and allow them to share in the profits of market making.

Steven Steinman and Rob Lazarowitz sold their highly successful business to our holding company, Roundtable Partners. Trimark is the second-largest third-market firm and currently does 25,000 to 30,000 trades daily. Their market share is between 1 percent and 2 percent of the NYSE volume. They sold their firm to Roundtable Partners for no money down and a small minority interest because they believed that the new combined entity would be far greater.

Throughout this process of building the firm and attracting partners we believed that success is a decision, not a circumstance. You know we never would have left our jobs if we wanted to open an ordinary OTC trading firm. From the very beginning we were convinced that if we assembled a group of highly talented traders and assistants, a top-notch support staff, a large order flow, and manage the firm imaginatively, we would be the largest and the best firm in the OTC market place. (*Note:* The OTC marketplace consisted of 550 competing market makers, including all of the large brokerage firms.)

All of you in this room were carefully selected from hundreds of candidates because we believe that you can make us the number one firm in the business. This is a formidable task, but if we all work harder and smarter than the competitors we can do it.

Why are we different?

1. Eleven of our owners are among the top 20 discount firms. The discount firms are the fastest-growing group of broker-dealers by a factor of three. That means they are growing three times faster than other groups such as regional firms. In addition, we are in serious discussions with three other large discount firms.

2. My partner Ken is the best that I know in the business. I would not have taken on this venture without him. Besides being one of the best traders, he is by far the best mentor in the business. Ken cares more about how successful his associates are than his own success.

3. When I was a partner at Herzog, Heine, Geduld, I helped build the largest correspondent network in the industry. My vision is that we will work

together to create an even larger correspondent network.

Another reason we are different is management style. In business it is very important to know your competitors. We know our competitors well.

1. One of them is managed by two individuals who have a contest to see who can take the most vacation time.

2. Another is managed by an individual who thought it would be OK to go into competition with his customers.

3. Another is managed by two individuals who are at the end of their careers and the new management is turning it into a corporate bureaucracy.

4. Another is managed by a highly successful individual, but he wants to make all the decisions himself and will not delegate responsibility. He believes, and he told his staff, that we are the biggest and most threatening competition to come along in their history.

We believe we have the opportunity to create a different and better firm. You would not be here if we didn't believe that you have what it takes to make this firm number one.

We did not form the Roundtable solely for monetary reasons. We were both very successful, but felt we could create an environment to allow employees to maximize both their earnings potential and feel good about where they were spending the majority of their lives.

We have a vision of what makes a firm great. And we understand why firms that could be great fail in reaching their potential.

Over the last 25 years I have worked for a number of firms that have taken short-cuts on the elements that are needed to be successful. I learned why their versions were destructive and ended with their firms failing to reach its full potential.

Backstabbing, office politics, inability to delegate responsibility, personal agendas, greed, hunger for power – these are the qualities that prevent a firm from reaching its full potential and make going to work unpleasant.

Ken and I want to set Knight apart from our competitors by creating the kind of environment which rewards teamwork, mentoring, honesty and integrity, and allows each individual to maximize his or her potential by openly learning and not being embarrassed to ask questions.

I have witnessed over and over how many of the trainees have lost their firms lots of money because they were afraid to ask a question that they thought might be perceived as stupid. It is important that everybody learn how to do everything right and I promise you that no one will ever be punished for asking a stupid question.

All of the individuals in this room were carefully selected, not only because of their trading ability, but also their ability to successfully work with all of our employees. We believe that the whole is greater than the sum of the parts – by working as a team we can accomplish far more than if we operate individually.

Ken and our staff spent an incredible amount of time selecting our trainees. Our trainees have great potential, but to develop that potential is going to require that the more experienced traders help in developing their raw talent. There is over 500 years of training experience in this room. Let's make a commitment to use it.

We want everyone in this room to be successful and feel good about themselves and come to work every day treating each other with respect. We will succeed in making a one-of-a-kind workplace.

I have shared with you how our firm was formed, how we are unique and the culture that sets us apart.

I would like those that believe that Knight Securities will be number one to stand up. I am going to count to three and we are going to shout at the top of our lungs: Knight is Number One!

While I told employees that day it would take two years, we actually got it done a lot quicker. In a period of 18 months my team and I created the largest firm of the 550 firms. In addition, I was also creating one of the fastest-growing firms of all times. On a capital base of $17 million we had $301 million in EBITDA in our fifth year.

How did we do it?

Mostly it came down to execution. When you are a market maker, you are the other side of every trade. That means taking risk. Which in turn means you need criteria for evaluating the risk inherent in every trade. We came out with the best execution criteria. We offered 5,000 share automatic executions on the top 2,000 NASDAQ stocks while our competitors offered only between 500 and 1,000 shares. This meant that if you sent your order of 5,000 shares or less to Knight the order would automatically be executed. This was a tremendous benefit, especially to the discount brokers who were transitioning into online brokers.

Our next unique service was to offer stop-loss protection on all NASDAQ stocks. This was a first in the industry, and our reasoning was that if the NYSE could offer it on listed securities we should do it for NASDAQ securities. This became an incredible success. None of our competitors wanted to offer it, but their customers demanded it. The result was that virtually every retail firm came to us with their stop-loss orders along with other business. IPOs were very popular and there were major complaints from the investors that they never received the opening price. We decided to guarantee the opening price and as a result received about 40 percent of all of the IPO order flow. Our next big step was to guarantee the opening price for all NASDAQ stocks. This was a highly successful service.

All of this shows how you can innovate and better serve customers if you can operate within the law but outside the yoke of unnecessary regulation. As I said, I doubt this could happen in the same way today, but it should be able to happen in the future if we're smart.

I'd also like to share another contemporaneous account from a neutral party, the magazine Traders, which wrote an approving and accurate article about us about a year into our development. This was a major turning point for us in gaining credibility within the industry. It's also kind of fun, with all the Knights of the Round Table imagery. There's also what now seems an ironic reference to one of our then-competitors – Bernie Madoff, who we met in the fraud chapter and whose demise is familiar to everybody.

Investment People[32]

The Knights of the Roundtable came as a 3 a.m. vision to Walter F. Raquet three years ago. As he tossed in the predawn hours, Raquet saw a crusade, not out of the trumpet-blowing medieval past, but out of an electronic trading, high-volume future.

Joining the crusade would be some of the toughest war horses in discount and regional brokerage, bent on reclaiming their NASDAQ order flow through internalization. They would name their endeavor Knight Securities, and build a 145-person, consortium-owned broker-dealer in the Newport Tower in Jersey City. And these Knights would metaphorically breathe life into the parent company, Roundtable Partners, LLC, with their order flow.

"We clearly saw a very bright future ahead," said Raquet, Knight's senior vice president of marketing. "The Knight's moniker resonated with the whole notion of high moral standards and a code of conduct, and it took us above the cult of personality, the notion of naming a firm after its owners."

Today, more than one year after its July 24th launch, Knight Securities is more than a vision turned into reality. It has become the fastest growing and arguably one of the most unique trading desks on Wall Street. It has also fulfilled its primary goal: Giving its partners more muscle in the marketplace.

To be sure, Knight represents a conquest for small broker-dealers lacking the economies of scale to develop their own over-the-counter desks. Yet, in terms of Wall Street priorities, Knight's charter has a noble purpose: To leverage the order flow and capital

---

[32] Reprinted from Traders magazine, September, 1996. Used with permission.

power of both its 25 brokerage firm owners and their retail customers.

Like the medieval Knights, there is honor and valor to uphold, though the routing of OTC order flow is essentially a good business decision. Nonetheless, as the rapid growth in trade volume demonstrates, these latter-day Knights have seen triumphs in their surging order flow reports. About 150 correspondents contribute their own volume, in addition to a growing institutional business, supported by 17 traders. The gambit is clearly working.

As of July, Knight Securities was averaging more than 20,000 trades daily – about 80 percent of them automated – a phenomenal growth rate compared to just over 3,600 daily trades about a year earlier. Nearly 90 percent of the business is retail. The firm projects handling up to 100,000 trades by the turn of the century.

Indeed, Knight Securities' trading armor has shined brighter with age. Its July trade volume represented 3.49 percent of overall NASDAQ trading volume, or nearly 20 million shares daily. The typical trade size is 1,000 shares. Knight said it supports that business with between $40 million and $50 million in overnight positions.

AutEx's volume rankings had Knight rising to seventh in July among broker-dealers, compared to 15th place in January. A year ago it ranked 88th.

Big and Small

The three top consortium members measured by order flow routed to Knight Securities are E-Trade Securities, Waterhouse Securities and Ameritrade. On the other end of the scale, smaller outfits like R.J. Forbes Group on Long Island generate roughly 5 percent of Waterhouse Securities' order flow. "There's no size or capital criteria for joining the consortium. All members are valuable," said Kenneth D. Pasternak, Knight's president and chief executive officer. Knight expects to close the consortium to new partners this month.

Consequently, Raquet sketched out a plan that would ultimately produce several benefits for the consortium owners and non-owners who routed their NASDAQ business to Knight.

These benefits range from lower execution costs to profit-sharing arrangements for consortium owners. In addition, Knight offers price improvement on more than 200 stocks, and price discovery and exposure on each limit order over 2,000 shares for both members and non-members.

"But basically, we wanted to level the playing field between the less powerful discounters and regionals that are on the rise, and their larger national competitors," Pasternak said.

Armed with a business plan, its own industry savvy and early financial backing from Waterhouse and others, Knight Securities set out to implement its strategy.

'We wanted to take control of the execution, to take control of our destiny and share proportionally from the profits and other economic benefits that derive from our arrangements at Knight," Pasternak said.

While Knight began trading in the technologically smart Newport Tower, Roundtable Partners simultaneously took over a listed trading desk, Trimark Securities, LP., in White Plains, N.Y.

Today, Knight may be one of the most profitable trading operations on Wall Street. The firm reports a 100 percent return on equity of $25 million. Knight has overall assets of $41 million. No wonder Knight officials are doing a little bit of Royal trumpet blowing.

"Just think about it, they were pouring the raw concrete for the floor in April 1995 and we started out with 75 employees," Raquet said. "Look where we're at today. We're making markets in more than 3,300 stocks, we have 145 employees, 42 of them market makers."

Back in 1993, the industry buzz was that Knight Securities' crusade had less to do with quality of execution, and more to do with the spotlight cast by the regulators on payment for order flow arrangements. One fear was that if the regulators banned payment for order flow, an important revenue stream would be suddenly lost. In that scenario, those potential losses – averaging 2 cents per share – could be stemmed by internalizing order flow.

Was payment for order flow a consideration? It would be "disingenuous" to deny it didn't play a role in the creation of Knight Securities, Pasternak said, "It had a bad connotation in the media, whereas if you have your own market-making unit, it gives a more favorable perception," he added.

Still, Pasternak insisted that payment for order flow wasn't the paramount concern. "I call it the economic value of an order flow resource," he said. "I would say payment for order flow wasn't really a driving force, it was the push for order flow centers to internalize execution."

As it turned out, the Securities and Exchange Commission eventually settled for disclosure on payment for order flow and didn't ban the practice. "The Commission actually came out and said payment for order flow was fine. It validated payment for order flow a year before our deal closed," Pasternak said.

Today, consortium and non-consortium members continue to receive those rebates: 2.5 cents per share on stocks priced $2.00 or more; 1 percent of principal on stocks under $2.00, and 2 cents per share on stocks in which Knight is not a market maker.

Of course, securities regulation requires firms engaged in payment for order flow arrangements to disclose if there is a price improvement mechanism for orders.

To be sure, there are some industry officials who think Knight Securities, like many good stories on Wall Street, will be consigned one day to the history pages, once the markets turn south.

Ready for Growth

But Pasternak and Raquet, both hardened veterans of the trading trenches, counter that Knight Securities is positioned for unprecedented growth.

By the turn of the century, Knight is confident it will be handling 100,000 trades daily.

More immediately, Knight estimates transaction volume over the next six months to grow between 25 percent and 75 percent. That increase, in part, is expected to come from a backlog of business routed by owners and prospective new owners, not to mention the efforts of heavy marketing. "We've conceptualized these numbers in our future. It's a realistic goal," Pasternak said.

He envisions growth also being fueled from a booming NASDAQ stock market. In plain mathematics, a 100,000 trade day would parallel 1 billion share days on NASDAQ.

Knight believes it has proven the critics wrong before. "They scoffed when we spoke of 25,000 trade days and we broke that last month," Pasternak said.

Count veteran securities industry analyst Perrin Long as one skeptic. "I wish them luck, but Charles Schwab never achieved those multiple increases in its trade volume," Long said. "If we have a half decent market over the next few years, maybe Knight could go to 50,000 trades daily."

Knight stands behind the 100,000 trades projection.

Over the next several months, Raquet counts an additional 10,000 average daily trades from "future correspondents" and that alone, he says, adds up to a 25 percent to 30 percent increase.

Pasternak sees a driving force behind Knight's growth coming from the discount brokerage industry. "Discounters are growing and taking more and more of the market away from full-line service firms," he said. "We see growth from our order flow centers growing at faster multiples than the market in general. We have had one owner growing at 10 percent a month in the past two years."

Behind Knight's success is a carefully conceived trading process, which has grown into a niche business that packs a competitive punch. Key to its strategy are its price improvement and price discovery products.

The price improvement mechanism works like this, according to an example the firm outlined. A client sends an order to buy 1,000 shares of XYC stock at the market (78-78¼). Knight stops the order at 78¼, while its proprietary system searches its open order book for a matching trade at a better price.

An open order exists for XYC stock at 78c and is filled on a share-by-share basis, in this instance, 600 shares. Then the trader searches orders residing on SelectNet but discovers no better price exists. The customer buys 600 shares of XYC stock at the improved price of 78c, and 400 shares at the stopped market price of 78¼.

Knight's price discovery mechanism on limit orders over 2,000 shares also protects Knight's traders from being SOESed on these orders, since the maximum SOES trade is 1,000 shares.

Other trading firms offer customer price improvement on their orders, among them Bernard L. Madoff Investment Securities. Firm principal Bernard Madoff, said his facility guarantees the customer the best price available on all stocks in which it makes a market. His firm's system automatically searches for better prices on SelectNet, while a trader simultaneously searches Instinet for price improvement. If there is no improved price, the system automatically adjusts the price inside the spread by half the spread, for instance c on active issues. The order then stays exposed for up to one minute. "The customer gets the best price," Madoff said. "That's substantially different [than Knight]," he added.

As noted, Knight does not execute all the order flow generated by its members and non-members. Ameritrade, for example, said trades are routed to Knight on a "symbol-by-symbol basis," based on the best execution – generally price improvement – available from several desks.

Ameritrade, whose customers transact about 50 percent of their retail orders via its PC-based Accutrade for Windows and touch-tone phone, plans to install an electronic routing system for its own correspondent brokers. This system will give correspondents greater control over the order entry and management process, including the designated order execution centers. However, Joseph A. Konen, president of Ameritrade's parent Transterra, is confident of Knight's ability to compete with the best.

But no business – no crusade, for that matter – ever occurred without shedding blood, sweat and tears. "To say that this was a cakewalk down a hill just wouldn't be true," Pasternak said, relating the nail-biting moments two weeks prior to Knight's opening.

"The SEC wouldn't give us our broker-dealer license unless we met some criteria," he said. "The conditions were absurd, and we reviewed them, and they reviewed them. Eventually they said,

'You're right,' and they allowed us to go ahead. It just got better and better from there on."

The 25 Knights

Ameritrade, Inc., Omaha, NE

BHC Securities Inc., Philadelphia, PA

BHF Securities, New York, NY

Bidwell & Co., Portland, OR

Brown & Co., Boston, MA

Burke, Christensen & Lewis Securities, Chicago, IL

Cowles Sabol, Encino, CA

Direct Access, Chicago, IL

E-Trade Securities, Palo Alto, CA

Gruntal Financial Corp., New York, NY

Hanifen Imhoff Clearing Corp., Denver, CO

Howe Barnes Investments, Chicago, IL

J.W. Charles Securities, Inc., Boca Raton, FL

Lombard Institutional Brokerage, San Francisco, CA

R.J. Forbes Group, Melville, NY

R.P. Assignee Corp., Jersey City, NJ

R.P.R. Gearing Services. St. Louis, MI

Richardson Greenshields, New York, NY

Sanders Morris Mundy, Houston, TX

Scottsdale Securities, St Louis, MI

Southwest Securities, Dallas, TX

Stockcross, Boston, MA

Thomas F. White & Co., San Francisco, CA

Van Kasper & Co., San Francisco, CA

Waterhouse Securities, New York, NY

As I said, this article was very helpful to us. But it was way too cautious. Instead of 100,000 trades we actually handled much more, including 2 million trades one day.

Many of our original partners wanted to go public so that their stake in the company could be monetized. Management wanted to go public so that our team could receive stock options and also increase our balance sheet in order to expand our institutional business. We also needed the capital to add new products and expand overseas. One of my proudest accomplishments is that we gave all 500 employees stock options and the value of those options for over 100 employees exceeded $1 million. Our administrative staff enjoyed options valued in the hundreds of thousands. Our regulators, in another stupid piece of regulation decided in 2003 to expense all stock options, which made it impossible to issue options as we did at Knight. The rule should have exempted smaller companies so that they could recruit and reward employees with options.

Larry Waterhouse suggested Bear, Stearns to handle our IPO. We were all excited and met with the senior staff at Bear, Stearns and were informed that they did not believe we could be a public entity. They felt that because a large amount of our order flow was coming from our partners, that would spook investors. We were disappointed but did not agree. We went to other firms and the response was different. They all wanted to do it and went out of their way to convince us to use them. In the end we choose BancBoston Robertson Stephens, Merrill Lynch & Co., PaineWeber Incorporated, ABN AMRO Rothschild, and Southwest Securities.

In July 1998 we went public and raised $145 million. One interesting story along the path to going public was a regulatory investigation into NASDAQ of the market makers. Our former firm Troster Singer was found to have been keeping trading spreads artificially high based on tape recorded conversations. Ken was accused of paying off someone as a result of those recordings, but it turned out to be his wife. The investigation was very helpful to Knight because we were a new firm and not involved and all of our competitors were up to their eyeballs in this investigation.

As we saw in the preceding chapter Arthur Levitt as head of the SEC hated NASDAQ because he tried to compete with them when he was at the Amex and got his butt kicked. Now he was seeking revenge.

His main weapons were electronic communication networks, or ECNs. The rise of ECNs can be attributed in large part to certain regulatory actions that helped create a favorable environment for the networks' entry into the equity markets. Levitt gave ECNs special privileges so they could screw the NASDAQ market makers, including Knight. NASDAQ market makers provided a two-sided market using risk capital. ECNs risked no capital, had electronic access to our markets, and were allowed to charge a commission. They were made legal and thrust into the market by regulatory decree. Were we in the United States or Russia? To add insult to injury, Levitt prohibited NASDAQ market makers from owning an ECN. Levitt was on his mission to punish NASDAQ and did not care who was hurt.

As we saw in the last chapter, NASDAQ announced that it would begin using a decimal pricing system, which would tighten the spreads at which we bought and sold stocks. As the market began to slow down and turned bearish, Knight's growth suffered as well. Our business model relied on volume and volatility, which were both in decline at the time. It was due to the SEC's new order handling rules, and the arrival of electronic trading systems which all negatively impacted profitability of all market making firms. This is what led Knight to expand into options market making as well as asset management.

Knight acquired Arbitrade as an expansion into the options market making Industry. Because of the volatility in NASDAQ markets, options were a very liquid market at the time. This proved a savvy move by Knight, because it increased revenue flows significantly. Arbitrade actively made markets in options on equities, equity indices, fixed income instruments, and certain commodities in the U.S.

I mentioned that our headquarters were in Jersey City, just across the Hudson from downtown Manhattan. That would prove especially significant on September 11, 2001.

During an executive meeting in our board room, which was right across the water and about a half a mile from the World Trade Center, we looked up and saw a hole in one of the towers, with a little bit of smoke. It was clear that a plane had flown into the trade center, and we were concerned that it was a terrorist act. As we were looking out at the Trade Center the most frightening image passed right before our eyes. A plane flew right past our office and turned and crashed into the second tower. Screaming, we made plans to evacuate. From outside our building we watched with heavy hearts as the towers burned, people jumped off the roof, and the first tower collapsed. Then the second one. It was horrific to witness.

Since all of Manhattan was closed off, I drove a number of employees who lived on Long Island up to Greenwich via the Tappan Zee Bridge. It was a somber ride. I started to reflect on my days at Cantor Fitzgerald, remembering those who were surely lost. Around sixty friends and colleagues passed away that day, six of whom I had hired during my time at Cantor.

One of them was Bill Tieste. I met Bill in 1968 when I was employed at Weeden & Co. Bill was a very bright accounting clerk who had dropped out of college. I mentored Bill and convinced him to go back and get his degree. After several years he received his degree and told me that my name should be on part of it because he never would have done it without my persistence. Shortly after he received his degree he was able to transfer into the equity trading department and become an institutional salesman, at which, gifted with an incredible personality, Bill became a highly successful. In the late 1970s when I was at Cantor Fitzgerald I recruited Bill to join the firm. I left in 1980 and Bill stayed on. I often reflect on that decision that cost Bill's life and devastated his family.

This was a galvanizing moment for many of the firm's original employees. Along with me, many of our employees had relatives and colleagues who worked in the World Trade Center. This caused an emotional bond to be formed among many people who were no more than acquaintances before the tragedy.

I left Knight in May the following year. I was fortunate enough to have collared several million shares of increasingly valuable Knight stock, which could have left me with a large tax liability. The way the tax law worked was that if I stayed employed by Knight I would have to pay ordinary income on my gain, but if I left it would be long-term capital gains, which as we've seen are taxed at a lower rate. The amount of money involved was between $5 million and $10 million, which made it unattractive for me to continue at Knight. This is another example of how our complex tax code forces behavior on us that we would rather not do.

Since my retirement, the Knight story has featured a number of twists and turns, which because I was no longer there I won't go into in detail.

After 2002 Knight was a $1.5 billion company that at one point handled 17 percent of the trades on both the NYSE and NASDAQ, making it by far the biggest trader of U.S. equities. It employed nearly 1,500 people. It got into trouble in 2012 when a programming error caused stock mispricing that ultimately cost the company $440 million in one day. Knight's stock collapsed and it barely survived. After a few failed rescue attempts, it was acquired by Getco LLC in 2013, and renamed KCG Holdings. But there is no question that the idea of high-speed trading we pioneered is here to stay.

"The situation for today's adults in their 30s and younger is particularly gloomy, with more storm clouds on the way, the researchers said. Their net worth relative to their parents is only about half what their parents' net worth was relative to their own parents.[33]" – Dallas Morning News

Chapter 8

HOW OVER-REGULATION IS DENYING MILLENNIALS THE SAME OPPORTUNITIES THEIR PARENTS HAD

"For many, the American dream of working hard, saving more, and becoming wealthier than one's parents holds true. Unless you're under 40." That's the grim finding of Eugene Steuerle, co-director of the Urban-Brookings Tax Policy Center, who co-authored the report, "Lost Generations? Wealth Building among Young Americans."[34]

I find this very troubling. What many people do not realize is that the world that we enjoyed and prospered in is not available to our children. Why is that? If you Google "younger generations fall behind their parents in wealth building" you will find 305,000

[33] http://bizbeatblog.dallasnews.com/2013/03/younger-generations-fall-behind-their-parents-inwealth-building.html/

[34] http://www.forbes.com/sites/ashleaebeling/2013/03/15/gen-x-and-gen-y-wealth-stagnates/#308173e9e42a

references. What is the reason for this? We have let the politicians ruin the American dream.

The politicians want to tax and regulate us to death and do not care about our livelihoods. They only care about lining their own pockets and their own future. They are very shortsighted and have no ability to plan for the future. They spend all their time on fundraising, running for re-election and coming up with crazy regulation.

I will give you an example of what I mean. Low economic growth is problem one, two and three. Do the politicians understand that? On March 7, 2016, there was an article in the *New Haven Register* announcing that Senators Richard Blumenthal (D-CT) and Charles Schumer (D-NY) are proposing to regulate the size of airline seats. Do these two morons not have anything better to do? The problem is that they are not focused or capable of participating in helping to increase GDP growth. There are thousands of examples of this type of stupid regulation. If someone does not like the size of the airline seat, they can choose another airline or go on a diet. Let the free enterprise system work.

It is time to stop all of this nonsense and create a government that works for all the people that want to work. How do we do this? We must take control of the process. The first step is to have business people on the board of directors of every government agency to make sure they do the right thing and to make these damn politicians accountable.

The next thing to do is to stop adding to, and begin reducing, our $19 trillion national debt. One of the most significant ways in which government debt hurts the economy is that it sacrifices the financial well-being of future generations. Allowing Congress to overburden citizens with debt in the present means that the next generation will have to come to grips with paying off trillions of dollars in obligations. Instead of putting their money into projects that grow the economy (job creation, investments, and savings), future tax-paying adults face the risk of higher tax rates, higher inflation, and a severe brake on economic growth.

Furthermore, massive debt is a symptom of government waste and unsound economic policies. Between 2009 and 2014, the federal government ran trillion-dollar deficits each year. During that time, the government lent $431 billion to protect otherwise failing financial institutions, authorized an $831 billion stimulus package, and continued to fund numerous wasteful and duplicative programs. These measures have taken resources out of a struggling economy and funneled them toward programs that give far less returns on the taxpayer's dollars than what free market investments would provide with those same dollars. Meanwhile, as we've seen, the middle-class hasn't had a raise in 15 years and it's been increasingly difficult for young people emerging from high-school or college to find a job.

Here are some staggering statistics:

1. Median Income: Millennials earned roughly $33,883 a year on average between 2009 and 2013 compared with $35,845 for their age group in 1980 and $37,355 in 2000 (all in 2013 inflation adjusted dollars.)
2. Staying Home: More than 30 percent of Millennials live with at least one parent, up from 23 percent in 1980 for the same age group, largely because they can't get a job.
3. Employment: Only about 65 percent of Millennials are currently working, compared with more than 70 percent of similar-aged kids in 1990.
4. Poverty: Almost 20 percent live in poverty, compared with about 14 percent in 1980.

If a business executive ran a company with this track record he would be fired.

Politicians need report cards. Helping to grow the economy is the most important item. They should be forced to report on what they have accomplished to help grow the economy. Regulating the size of airline seats should get an F.

Again, this is not a Democratic or a Republican problem. Barack Obama and George W. Bush both have lousy track records on regulation. According to a Heritage Foundation report by James L. Gattuso and Diane Katz in May 2015, there had been 184 major new regulations through 2014 under Obama at an estimated cost of $80 billion. George W. Bush enacted 76 new regulations costing $30.7 billion, according to Heritage.

This why the economy cannot grow.

In my opinion that should be the number one question in the 2016 Presidential race. How are they going to get rid of all the economy-killing regulation?

It is important to educate Millennials about the dangers of over-regulation and make them understand that their future is being robbed by the regulation-crazy politicians.

In my view, we're never going to be able to leave a better country, or even one with the level of opportunity we all enjoyed, to our children and grandchildren unless we do some fundamental house-cleaning. We need to sweep away most regulation, install boards of directors to run government agencies like efficient businesses and reward whistleblowers to eradicate fraud in government and private companies. This will go a long way toward solving our most insidious problem, that of runaway government debt.

Ultimately, debt is driven by an unhealthy addiction to spending. Tax increases have been suggested as a solution to reducing the national debt, but such proposals would just hurt an already weak economy. In the end, spending cuts and responsible budgeting are the only pro-growth solutions to America's massive debt crisis. In the end, America is deeply in debt because politicians spend too much, not because families and businesses are taxed too little.

And of course there's the specific Millennial problem of frequently being saddled with a huge amount of student debt. This is often a combination of being unable to find part-time jobs and tuition, and fees rising at several times the rate of inflation and much faster than the stagnant wages of their parents. Natalie Kitroeff, writing for Bloomberg News in December 2015, said all this debt is dampening home-buying, which hurts everyone from builders to Procter & Gamble to Campbell's Soup; delays them starting a family, which is bad news for crib and diaper manufacturers; prevents them from saving as much as they should, bad for banks and the whole economy; and impairs their finances for a long while to come.

We owe it to our children and grandchildren to start fixing this problem now.

I hope this book educates Millennials about the dangers of big, reckless government. The free market system works. America is the greatest country in history and it was built on the free market system. Government is necessary but should be limited to providing the necessities for a free society. Socialism has never worked anywhere. As Margaret Thatcher liked to say: "The problem with Socialism is that you eventually run out of other people's money."

There is no free lunch! Wake up and vote for freedom!

"Do you want to bet the $50,000?" –
The author, on whether a new trading system would work, 1980

Chapter 9

PERSONAL EXPERIENCES WITH ENTREPRENEURSHIP AND BUCKING THE SYSTEM

When I argued in the previous chapter that today's youth is at a disadvantage compared to my generation, I was specifically thinking of times in my past when, either ignorant of or unfettered by pervasive rules and regulations, I was able to make a difference for myself and for the businesses I worked for, and by extension, for the economy and country as a whole. I deeply believe this isn't possible now, but I also deeply hope that by instituting the reforms I'm proposing in this book, we can get back to a time of prosperity.

My dad was truly a blessing. He taught me so many things. I owe much of my success to him. I want to share with you some of the qualities that made him such a special man.

Hard work – My dad could outwork anyone I've ever met. No one could ever keep up with him. When he was 75 and I was 42, I finally caught up to him. My dad had incredible energy and physical strength. My dad was a fireman but always had other jobs. He and a friend of his would buy foreclosed houses and fix them up and sell them. When I was about 14 my father asked me if I would like to make $10 for 2 hours of work (at that time minimum wage was about 85 cents an hour). I said sure. He took me to an office building and told me to carry the roofing supplies up to the roof. There were 100 pieces weighing about 55 pounds each that I had to carry up a 30-foot ladder. I learned quickly that I wanted to use my head to make money.

Honor – My father taught me that the only thing you have that can never be taken away is your honor.

Investing – My dad bought me my first stock when I was eight. I was proud to own stock. He was a very savvy investor who did very well over the years, and although he never made a lot of money working, he was able to accumulate $1 million.

At age 16 I decided to become an entrepreneur. I sent away for catalogs for wedding invitations, calendars and other advertising materials along with Christmas cards. I would go door-to-door to businesses and try to sell them anything from matchbooks to calendars. My friends all had jobs at the local supermarket making a dollar an hour. I was able to make approximately $10 an hour by running my own business. Some days, I would make nothing; other days, I would make $100 to $200. Through teaching myself, I was able to learn how business works. I remember one particular incident very well, I was about to sell a delicatessen owner $400 worth of calendars and my commission was $120, when his wife arrived on the scene and wanted to change the picture on the calendar. Unfortunately, I made the big mistake of siding with the wife's choice. An argument started and I was asked to leave with no sale. The lesson: the customer's always right, but first you've got the figure out who the customer is!

Being an entrepreneur doesn't always mean selling calendars or starting your own restaurant. Often you can be an entrepreneur within a big organization by displaying the key element of entrepreneurship: independent thinking.

For example, I joined Paine Webber as their corporate controller in 1980, a classic staff job of the sort that many people get and quietly occupy until they retire, making no waves. They had just completed an acquisition of Blythe Eastman Dillon and the accounting records were a disaster. Bank accounts and trading accounts in some cases had not been reconciled in months. The auditors at Ernst & Young were not going to give an opinion on the books, a disaster which would have forced the company to liquidate. I worked 45 straight days, and with the help of the accounting staff and 75 temporary workers, we were able to get the records in order.

In my sixth week there, Dugald Fletcher, who was the vice chairman of the company and responsible for systems and operations, came to my office and said he wanted to make me the chief financial officer and get rid of Jack Rivkin, the current CFO. I told him I had been working every day for the last 45 days, that my mission was to get the company through the audit, and that I had no time for politics. About a week later he announced that he wanted to shut down the GNMA business of Paine Webber, which involved trading mortgage securities backed by Ginnie Mae and was generating about $10 million of the $50 million in profits of the entire firm. I happened to be an expert in the GNMA business, coming from Cantor Fitzgerald, which was also a major mortgage-backed securities trader. In fact, I had helped develop a very sophisticated system while I was there, and I suggested that we could use the Cantor Fitzgerald system to fix PaineWebber's problems. I had already spoken to the people at Cantor Fitzgerald and they agreed to lease us use of the system for $20,000 a month.

Fletcher said that he would send his systems group over to evaluate the system at Cantor Fitzgerald, a classic ploy of entrenched bureaucrats when their turf is threatened. About a week later I got a call phone call from Jack Rivkin, who was my boss and one of the best people I have ever worked with, and whom I had declined to unseat a while previously. He said Fletcher wanted to meet with us, so Jack and I met with Fletcher in the vice chairman's very large office at about 5:30 in the evening. Dugald looked at me and said that his systems people evaluated the system at Cantor Fitzgerald, and that it would never work and that I was full of shit.

In those days we used to call this type of event a nuke attack. It took me about 30 seconds to collect my thoughts. I looked at him straight in eye and said I'm going to come in tomorrow and put 50 thousand dollars in cash on your desk and bet you and those assholes that work for you that I'll install the system in eight weeks without any of your help, and I will save the GNMA business. Dugald looked at Jack. The vice chairman was in shock and didn't know what to do. Finally, after a few minutes, he put his head down, grabbed his desk drawer and started opening and closing it and rocking back and forth in his chair. He started humming, and then said "meeting over, meeting over, meeting over." Jack and I looked at each other, got up and left the meeting.

We went straight over to the office of Don Marron, the chairman of PaineWebber, and told him the story. Marron looked at me and asked, "Do you think the system will work?" I replied: "Do you want to bet the $50,000?" He, to his credit, said to just put the system in. Six weeks later Paine Webber's GNMA business was saved.

Prior to joining PaineWebber I worked for Weeden & Co., another big Wall Street firm. When I left Price Waterhouse to go to Weeden I quickly discovered that being bright and graduating at the top of my class did not matter. It was all about connections and relationships. No firm would hire me for the front office and the only opportunities were the back office. I decided to join Weeden & Co. because of their size – Weeden was the 10th largest brokerage firm in the U.S. When I joined Weeden I had to work 60 straight days, because they had understated their financial record keeping problems. They had not reconciled 75 of their bank accounts for the preceding nine months, and the regulators were going to close them down unless the financial reporting was fixed. I assembled a small team and in six weeks we brought the books up to date. During my first two years I implemented four of the following ideas that saved Weeden $2 million a year. For a company with profits of $10 million that was very significant.

I believe my ideas about boards of directors for government agencies and rewarding whistleblowers could save this country between 5 percent and 10 percent of its spending, or between $190 billion and $380 billion a year. I advanced quickly and was corporate controller by age 26. I tell these stories not to brag, but rather to illustrate what innovative thinking can do when not burdened by regulation. This should go on everywhere, all the time!

The first idea for Weeden was the flyaway program. Weeden had a lot of securities that had to be delivered to major out-of-town banks and they would be sent by courier. (There was no email then.) I discovered that sometimes it would take between three days and five days for these securities to reach the reach the designated bank. I calculated the interest and the value of the securities and came to the conclusion that that in some cases where the dollar amounts were so high, we could actually fly a messenger out and then we would get paid Fed funds that day. In the first year of the flyway program the company saved approximately $600,000.

Second was the late-delivery program. Securities were delivered by messenger and had to be at the banks, which were all located in the Wall Street area, by 11:30 a.m. If they weren't delivered by 11:30 a.m. the securities had to be delivered the following day by that time. Interest rates were around 8.5 percent and delivering the next day cost Weeden $300 per every million dollars of securities. If, for example, you had a $5 million delivery of securities that missed the 11:30 a.m. deadline, it would cost Weeden $1,500 to carry it until the following day. If it was a Friday it would cost the company three days' interest, or $4,500. I decided to build a network of relationships with the branch managers of these Wall Street banks so that we could make late deliveries. We had dinners and lunches with these managers over the following four weeks and in the month after that we were able to make late deliveries on large orders. In the first twelve months we saved Weeden $700,000.

Next, I looked at how long our checks took to clear. Weeden issued checks for large amounts to many huge financial institutions. I observed that these checks often took three days to five days to clear. However, we didn't have to have money in the bank to cover them until they cleared. I had two employees analyze the checks we issued for more than $100,000 to financial institution for the previous 12 months to determine how long these checks were outstanding. Using this information, I could allow Weeden's bank accounts to be overdrawn during the month on our books until the checks cleared. I was able to generate a daily float of $20 million to $40 million during each month, which saved the company from having to borrow the money at 8.5 percent. The savings to Weeden was over $1 million annually. This process had to be carefully managed. If it wasn't it could cause significant overdrafts.

Lastly I had an idea how we might legally save some tax money. The state of New York taxed all transactions that took place in New York. I spoke to our attorneys and verified that if the customer was out of the state and they agreed to the price, then the transaction was deemed to be an out-of-state transaction and no tax was due. Weeden did about 10 percent of the NYSE volume. The savings could be significant if I trained the traders on the large transactions to have the customer accept the price and note it on the trade ticket. On a daily basis I would review the large tickets to make sure they were being filled out correctly. The savings was about $75,000 per month. One day I noticed that a large trade was filled out incorrectly and it cost us $1,500. I went to the trader and explained that he just cost us $1,500 by being careless. He started screaming at me and told me I did not know what I was talking about. We were on the trading floor with about 75 people looking at us and I responded, "How much do you want to bet?" He backed down fast and I earned a lot of respect from the other traders.

I mentioned in Chapter 5 that after my whistleblowing experience at Sentinel Financial, I was basically left to my own devices to innovate and try to create a business. Here's what happened.

The seeds were planted in my mind when I was at market-maker Herzog Heine Geduld in 1980. They were doing everything manually, including writing out trading tickets and giving them to key punch operators who would then enter those tickets into the system. So we were trading large sums of money, but we really never knew where we were, and we would have people looking at all those tickets and trying to keep track of the various ownership positions. They were called scribes – and they would try to post the records to let the traders know how much they were either long – offering to buy shares – or short – offering to sell them.

One day I came across two individuals: Craig Conte and Paul Femeno, who had access to then-brand-new computer system called Stratus, and they had used it to schedule and track deliveries for a busy dairy. This was the second fault-tolerant computer on the market. It didn't crash as many earlier models frequently did. I really liked the hardware and I liked these guys. They were very bright and had developed a complex system that involved loading up trucks and delivering milk and cheese to neighborhoods all over New England -- many different drop-offs. They had figured out how instruct the computer how to load the trucks so that everything would be in the right order. This was a big deal at the time. I liked the fact that they could do something so complex and they'd had some experience doing some Wall Street back-office systems.

So the three of us set out to create a sophisticated Wall Street trading system. Nobody told us we could do this, but nobody told us we couldn't. If there were thousands of pages or regulations governing what we could do and what we couldn't do, we didn't know about them and wouldn't have let them get in the way in any event.

We invented a lot of new bells and whistles for traders that hadn't been done before. With our system we could make the back office of every trading shop cost-effective. One of the things I insisted on, which we did, was to store all the stock positions and profit and loss statements in the computer's memory. In most cases these were still being kept in hand-written ledgers by those poor scribes. Now with the computer, when the trader needed information he or she could pull it right up and didn't have to wait; it came right at them. Again, a big deal in 1984.

This also allowed the firm's management to know on a real-time basis exactly how much risk they were taking, and the traders knew the jumping-off point of every trade. At the time it was the most sophisticated equity trading system in the world. It took us about six months to complete the programing and roll it out initially. It took approximately another three months to install it at

Herzog. At that time Herzog was doing about 2 percent of all the trades on the NASDAQ, I also then got permission to sell the software to other firms, and we ended up selling it to 21 of the 30 largest firms in the world. Our first outside sale was to Goldman Sachs, which gave us a lot of credibility. But even here, the bureaucrats had their say. Goldman Sachs spent more money evaluating the system than they paid for it.

We called the system COLT (for Continuous On-Line Trading system), and in competition with other such systems, it went on to be used by many firms. Now all this technology is commonplace.

COLT boosted our business by more than 200 percent, from about 2 percent of NASDAQ trading to 6 percent, adding as much as $30 million to our annual profits. I think it's safe to say it revived my career after the dark days of Sentinel. And I continue to view it as a triumph of innovation over regulation. We didn't worry about the rules; we of course stayed within them, but changed the business, and by extension, the financial system. And yes, in areas like technology this sort of thing still happens. But we need it to happen everywhere, every day, and that's not going to be possible until we get rid of the shackles holding us back.

More recently, at the age of 71, I've become involved as an advisor to a young company called AtmosAir that has developed a revolutionary process to filter room air.

AtmosAir's revolutionary product cleans the air by eliminating odors, volatile organic compounds, mold and mildew, dust and bacteria and viruses. It enables commercial facilities to reduce using outside air by 50 percent, which results in substantial electrical savings. Depending on its location the system will pay for itself in 18 to 36 months. For example, in Florida our customers have been getting an 8 percent total reduction in their electric bill.

The company has been in business for 10 years, is profitable and has over 7,000 installations. There is 88 billion square feet of commercial real estate in the U.S. alone that needs this product, in addition to the government, schools etc., and the rest of the world.

I met Steve Levine, the CEO, at a breakfast in July 2015 and he told me about the company. I told him what he needed to do to take his company to the next level. Some of the items were to outsource his manufacturing and arrange financing for the sales, which we have accomplished. We are now raising $5 million to build out the sales force, and I have little doubt this can become a billion dollar company someday.

"It's not in the dreaming, it's in the doing." –
Mark Cuban, as seen on YouTube

Chapter 10

HOW TO INSPIRE INDIVIDUALS TO BECOME SUCCESSFUL ENTREPRENEURS

I have learned a lot during my career about what makes a person or a company successful. I want to pass my thoughts about success to the readers of this book.

1. I always approached my job with the attitude that if I were the president how would I make the company a better place.

2. If you are the president you have to know how everything works; I always tried to understand everything.

3. If you do not know something, do not be afraid to say you do not know it. Credibility and integrity are critical to success. The phonies get weeded out very fast, although sometimes not fast enough.

4. You must read the Wall Street Journal, five years of reading WSJ is like getting an MBA.

5. Learn how to become a public speaker; while we all have some degree of natural skills, practice makes perfect.

6. You must never be afraid to fail. Learn from your failures. If you never get up to bat you will never hit a home run.

Abe Lincoln said, "Things may come to those who wait, but only the things left over by those who hustle."

7. Take pride in your conduct and appearance.

I have recently been introduced to an amazing company called Koru (JoinKoru.com) by CEO and founder Kristen Hamilton. Koru has introduced a scientific approach for employers to make better hires and for employees to find what they are best suited for.

The Koru Seven – seven components for measuring how individuals will perform in their jobs – was developed as a result of decades of research by global experts. The Seven are:

1. GRIT - The ability to stick with it when things get hard. When directions are not explicit, identifying hires who can make sense of ambiguous situations. Key traits are Grit; Growth Mindset; Self-Efficacy.

2. OWNERSHIP - Positive and empathetic hires can be a joy to work with, contributing to great teams – being able to not only do work in service of others, but also take initiative when things are not clear to help early career talent stand out. Traits are Proactivity; Citizenship; Integrity; Conscientiousness.

3. CURIOSITY - Beyond simply asking why, curiosity can also spark innovation. Hires that are curious, not only about their product or role, but also about the roles of others, or competitive products, tend to be better informed, have a better eye for detail, and often ask the right questions. Creativity; Empathy.

4. POLISH - No matter your role, being an effective communicator is important for co-workers and clients like. From writing effective emails to asking thoughtful questions, workers with Polish are great collaborators. Communication.

5. TEAMWORK - There are no dark corners in organizations anymore. Everyone must collaborate to produce work and drive results. Even software developers work in teams. Emotional Intelligence; Collaboration; Positivity.

6. RIGOR - Innovative companies care about data in all areas, so we screen for the ability to read, interpret and process data quickly and in a detail-oriented way. Evidence-Based Decision-Making.

7. IMPACT - Great early hires not only can do the duties in their role, but they also understand their contribution and impact to the larger organization's objectives. Hires with Impact are efficient, and think about the company's success instead of just their own. This leads to real-world problem solving and innovation.

That's how individuals should behave to succeed, but how should companies behave to succeed?

1. Build a business that all the employees believe in.
2. Set the quality of your production of goods or services high. Aim to be the best.
3. Understand your competition.
4. Run the company on a fiscally conservative basis.
5. Set up a customer-focused culture.
6. Embrace technology.
7. Share profits with your employees and make them feel like they are part of the team.
8. Communicate as much as you can.
9. Talk about your successes.
10. Keep the spirit up and positive.

This chapter didn't talk explicitly about regulation, unlike the rest of the book, but the implicit message is the same. People and the companies they work for, be they Millennials or Fortune 500, Baby Boomers or the corner donut shop, need to be able to grow and thrive by acting in their own interests and those of their employees and customers. They must be spared spending all day filling out forms, worrying that they might have broken a rule. If they see something wrong and report it they should be praised rather than fired.

We need more entrepreneurs, not fewer, and they need fewer regulations, not more.

"You don't learn to walk by following rules. You learn by doing, and by falling over." – Richard Branson as quoted by Brainy Quotes

Chapter 11

KEEP AMERICA GREAT – BY CHANGING THE RULES

Let's look back a bit and then look forward.

We saw right from the start that slow growth is the overriding economic issue of our time and the middle class hasn't had a raise in 15 years. Meanwhile, government employees kept getting raises above and beyond their private sector colleagues

My conviction, of which I hope I've convinced you, too, is that in large part this has been caused by stifling over-regulation by government that keeps companies from reaching their full potential in innovation and job creation, and discourages the brightest people from starting their own businesses, as I was fortunate enough to do.

I've shown that government regulations, the inefficient presidential (Bush and Obama) administrations, and out-of-control spending are to blame. Remember the 74,000 pages of IRS regulations and the 20,000 more dumped on businesses by Obamacare? Remember the $2 trillion cost?

That was the starting point for my proposing real and practical reforms. At their heart is the fundamental idea of running the federal government like a business, not to make some sort of paper profit, but rather to operate as efficiently as a successful private company, eliminating all the nonsense. Boards of directors won't tolerate nonsense.

To review the concept, each board would hire industry experts to apply the best and most efficient business practices to a failing and wasteful system, hire and fire, and trim obsolete rules and functions. Nothing is going to change until we can get rid of the harmful and needless regulations that are strangling our businesses.

The second part of the solution is to unleash the millions of whistleblowers who go to work every day and see ridiculous, sometimes criminal, stuff going on and are either too scared or simply not motivated to report it. No, this isn't a standard politician's promise to get rid of fraud, waste and abuse, though I'm certainly all for getting rid of those things. This is a very practical proposal that will actual stop waste, fraud and abuse and save the American taxpayer billions of dollars a year. I know this because, as you've seen, I was a whistleblower, though unrewarded; and welcome though imperfect, the SEC program has already netted billions of dollars.

Far from being a doomsayer, I'm optimistic that if we can get boards of directors running the government and help whistleblowers police the system, the world's largest economy and the world's greatest country can soar again.

My plans aim to unleash business creation, education, employment, capital markets, efficient energy and immigration. These are the engines that allow people to innovate, create and benefit from their efforts without government interference and hindrance.

We all need a strong, vibrant economy which will give the middle class their long-delayed raise and enable the taxpayer to provide the government with funding to ensure our safety, the promise of acting in the best interest of the people, and to protect the environment.

But how can any of this actually get done?

Without citing any specific candidate, I would suggest that all voters look for candidates at all levels who seem open to fresh ideas. Write opinion pieces, get involved in local campaigns, call your representatives offices and present them the facts. Give them a copy of this book, if you like.

And yes, it's okay to be angry at what's gone on in our government for far too long, as long as that anger is directed toward change. Take my ideas, add to them, use them to convince and persuade.

Let me be absolutely clear once again. I am not advocating breaking the rules – as you've seen I have, often at great personal cost, blown the whistle on lots of people whom I've seen breaking the rules. I'm talking about *changing* the rules. That's a lot harder and it's going to take a multi-level effort by all of us to make it happen.

While the ideas I've outlined are simple to understand, I have no illusion that they will be simple to implement. But it shouldn't be impossible. A president of either party comes into office fired up about reforming government and forging a new path. Appointing bi-partisan boards and enlisting the best and the brightest has a long history reaching back to John F. Kennedy and beyond.

It's up to all of us to talk about and promote these ideas with whatever influence we have. If you're on social media, help me make these ideas go viral. I've posted some ideas on how to do this, as well as a number of related thoughts and news articles, on this book's website, deregulateamerica.com. If you go to a lot of cocktail parties or belong to a book club or to candidate town halls, I've given you a rich topic of conversation.

Writing this book has opened my eyes to a lot of things that shocked and surprised me, but ultimately showed me that America is great, and to keep it so we need to change a lot of things, However, it also has convinced me more than ever that together we can do it.

Let's get started.

ABOUT THE AUTHOR

Walter Raquet is a leader whose innovations and values have had a profound effect on American business.

Mr. Raquet uncovered the largest tax fraud ($1 billion) in the history of the United States and assisted the U.S. Treasury and the IRS in shutting it down. (1980)

He created the first sophisticated equity trading system, called COLT, which was used by the majority of the world's trading firms. (1984)

In 1995, he founded a company with $17 million in capital and 70 employees. In its fifth year, the company had EBITDA of $301 million, employed 1,400 people and its public value rose as high as $8 billion. (1995-1999)

Mr. Raquet during that period predicted that asinine regulation by Arthur Levitt, then the chairman of the Securities and Exchange Commission, would gravely harm the capital markets. Levitt's over-regulation caused the loss of 18 million jobs in the U.S. over a 15-year period.(1997)

At the age of 26, Walter Raquet was the corporate controller of the 10th largest Wall Street firm. Today, at the age of 71 he is guiding the CEO of AtmosAir, a company that cleans the air and reduces energy use dramatically, to make that firm grow to a multi-billion-dollar enterprise in the next three years.

Made in the USA
Middletown, DE
26 February 2019